THE REVELATION OF THE FATHERHOOD

PLAN OF GOD FOR EVERYONE

ELOU FLEURINE

Copyright © 2021 by Elou Fleurine (MBA)

All rights reserved. No part of this publication may be reproduced, distributed, or transmitted in any form or by any means, including photocopying, recording, or other electronic or mechanical methods, without the prior written permission of the author, except in the case of brief quotations embodied in critical reviews and certain other noncommercial uses permitted by copyright law. Permission will be granted upon request.

All Scriptures quotations in the book are from the New King James Version of the Bible. Scripture Quotations marked KJV are taken from King James Version of the Holy Bible. All Greek and Hebrew from the strong Bible Dictionary.

THE REVELATION OF THE FATHERHOOD

For information contact:
1001 NE 15 ST
Homestead, FL 33030
http://www.kingjesush.org

Book and Cover design by Digital Publishing of Florida
ISBN: 978-1-949720-81-5

First Edition: February 2021

CONTENTS

INTRODUCTION 5

1. Spiritual Paternity 18
2. Responsibility of the Spiritual Parents 32
3. The Model of Fatherhood 40
4. Fatherhood and Sonship 49
5. Lack of Fatherhood and Crisis of Spiritual Direction 57
6. Understanding the Power Behind the Fatherhood 65
7. Fatherhood the Plan of Growth 72
8. How To Honor Spiritual Parents? 83
9. Mentor and Spiritual Father 101
10. The Necessity for a Church to be Under a Spiritual Covering .. 109
11. Spiritual Fatherhood Breaks Barriers 123

12. Covering Reveals Purpose 133

13. Fatherhood and Responsibility 141

14. The Fatherhood With Guillermo Maldonado 157

Conclusion 164

DEDICATION 167

INTRODUCTION

Spiritual Fatherhood is one of the subjects that has become popular in our spiritual environment, especially in the apostolic ministries.

The issue of spiritual fatherhood is so fundamental in this time of revival prompting in Church advancement. The point is predominant because the body of Christ needs true fathers and true mothers to create healthy and mature children. Although we speak, then, of spiritual fatherhood, we also include the ministry of some women as spiritual mothers within the body of Christ. Therefore, we conceive of spiritual fatherhood as fatherhood and motherhood, but we will speak of spiritual fatherhood for reasons of convenience.

There have been critical spiritual movements in the church's history: The Protestant Reformation, The Pentecostal Movement or The Reformation of the Holy Spirit, and The

Apostolic Reformation. They have all influenced it to bring it back to the original intent. We also call these revivals or movements of the Holy Spirit "reforms" because each one of them has brought profound changes in the mental structure of the church; at the head of these reform movements, there have been men of God who have been the pioneers and considered the spiritual promoters and fathers in these processes of God.

The apostolic reform brings the Father's revelation to the center of the church's life, to the very scene of the Christian spiritual experience. One of the most important pillars that this apostolic reform brings for the church to live and proclaim it is the Father's revelation. (Hebrews 1: 1) *"God having spoken to parents many times and in many ways through the prophets; in these last days he has spoken to us by the Son."*

The revelation of the spiritual Father decodes life in the human spirit generating changes in all areas of the work of men and women. It is important to note that having the Father's revelation is not the same as having biblical knowledge. If so, then many very lucid atheists or religious in biblical knowledge could thoughtlessly be transformed into a new life. They have not altered Satan himself, who deftly quoted the scriptures to the Lord Jesus. In our day, there are learned Muslims with impressive biblical knowledge, which is skillfully employed to debate — and even embarrass — Christians themselves, yet that knowledge does not generate inner life.

There are many supposedly Christian people in churches

today, even in leadership positions, who certainly have biblical knowledge but lack the spiritual Father's revelation. It is the reason why so much scandal is observed among the Christian people.

Only Christ has brought us the sole and absolute revelation and knowledge of the Father. He came from the very bosom of the Father. He came from the same glory of the Father and communicated to us his Word, his Purpose, and manifested to us. He said," *I and the Father are one* "(John 6:46).

Nowadays, more and more priests, nuns, and even laypeople are asked to be "spiritual father." It must be understood that this process manifests a real desire to direct their life more towards Christ and progress on the path of holiness.

When speaking of spiritual fatherhood, it is necessary to remember that above all things, all of us who have received Christ as Lord of our life are children of God. This relationship is above any other parenting relationship, including the natural parenting relationship.

Spiritual fatherhood as practiced by Jesus and the first Christians consisted essentially in transmitting spiritual teaching, leading the disciples to perceive who is God, who is the Father - this is the object of all the Parables. It also consisted of leading someone to the heart's purity by putting them before the obligation to take radical decisions. It also consisted of the example of a life of service (Jesus washing the feet of the Apostles).

Today in life, the conjecture is often deadly. Crisis after crisis, we are now living in perilous times and are most demanding because of the Enemy! Without a guide, a spiritual father, you are likely to go amiss! Therefore, the relationship with the Spiritual Father is not just any relationship where one is content to discuss. It is a meeting where I put myself under God's regard to get to know myself better and thus be always more faithful to Him, accepting on my part a genuine conversion to put Christ at the center of my existence. We can see this relationship places us in what is most fundamental in our life as a man and a Christian, and therefore that we cannot stop at a simple exchange.

The Church has always recommended that Christians who wish to advance in their journey have recourse to a spiritual father. Since no one is a good judge of himself, God uses this channel to escort you and speak to you.

Everyone who occupies a leading position in the local Church receives delegated authority as the local Church's spiritual Father. The people who congregate in that local Church are the spiritual sons and daughters of that spiritual Father.

God places in that spiritual Father an inheritance for his spiritual sons and daughters (See Isaiah 59:21). Spiritual sons and daughters receive a double portion of that inheritance (like Elisha with respect to Elijah, and the disciples with respect to Jesus, (See John 14:12).

The assistants, the members, the sheep, and the disciples, the male or female servants, do not receive the inheritance. Sons and daughters only receive the inheritance.

We can live in the house and not be children (like the

prodigal son and his brother, who, as natural children, did not feel like real children; they had the mentality of day laborers, (See Luke 15: 11-31).

To receive the inheritance God has placed for us as spiritual sons and daughters, we need to learn to live like his sons and daughters.

In the church's life, the establishment of God's authority is a vital concern. Because the subject of spiritual leader has been distorted some within the Lord's retrieval and outside, a proper understanding of spiritual father or authority is greatly needed.

When God delegates authority, the authority He delegates is an authority of a paternal nature because he is Father and his authority is Paternal. God delegates authority on at least three levels:

- The family: the natural father.
- The church: the spiritual parents.
- The government: the parents of the country.

When God delegates his authority, in addition to equipping the delegates so that they can exercise that authority well, he also provides them with an inheritance for the sons and daughters who will be under his care. Always, a father of a family, a spiritual one, has an inheritance for his sons and daughters in those instances.

God created man in His image, giving him the freedom to know Him and love Him. This initiative freely taken by God requires the same freedom in your response. Indeed, it is free that the soul can love and enter dialogue with God. Now, if you want to know and love God more every day, you must be faithful to Him. This is precisely what spiritual father tends to do: to give you the right means to grow in spiritual life.

In the New Testament, no one can set himself above the authority of the body and claim to represent God's authority if a brother is unwilling to have his work blended with others and is unwilling to bring his work into the common prayer and fellowship of the co-workers, that one's work is not under the authority of the Head. The authority of the throne is with those who have a clear sky (See Ezekiel 1:26). When a person with spiritual authority contacts people, he does not need to vindicate himself or assert his own authority because the presence and witness of the Spirit are there. Because the Spirit Himself is there, the authority of the Spirit also is there.

It is incredible for a church or a believer to live without a spiritual father. We need in this generation spiritual parents in our churches that can teach us... obedience, character, humility, and passion. It is important that spiritual fatherhood be restored. In difficult times, a spiritual father is necessary. He is one who watches over you.

Ministers were frustrated that they were made in unsubstantiated denominations and without spiritual parenting. You need a father to correct you. In addition, you need to give an account to someone.

You must understand that your spiritual father does not gain anything. He is there to help you, to listen to you, and in no case to make decisions for you. He is the doctor of your soul: if you do not tell him sincerely your difficulties and your doubts ... he will neither be able to guess them nor help you.

Many Church leaders or believers who are orphans with no proper spiritual father soon die spiritually. Fatherhood is in the heart of God. He made us live as a family so that the Fathers take care and teach the fruit of their womb. This is as valid in the natural as in the spiritual. God wants to validate in us the promises made to Abraham: I will give you offspring. God has put in us a very powerful seed that, when put into action, multiplies with enormous potential.

Paul clearly understood the importance of spiritual fatherhood, he not only understood it, but he practiced it. He called Timothy a true son in faith. (See 1 Timothy 1: 2)

Spiritual fatherhood is part of our identity; it runs like DNA through our veins, it defines us as believers, it identifies us as heirs to the kingdom; we may have many children, but we only have spiritual parents.

To be a father, you must first be a son. It is in the acceptance of this filiation that all paternity flourishes before being transmitted again. Becoming a father means registering yourself in a genealogy, communicating life in turn. Being a father is not a title; it is a mission and a fight for life. Today, if we see a devaluation of the paternal model, it is above all a deep rejection of references that are not adjusted to the truth of this vocation to give life and make it grow.

The potential and responsible prophetic fatherhood are founded on the graces of baptism, rooted in the death and resurrection of Christ. When we are immersed in the water of baptism, we become priests, prophets, and kings. We are not in a palliative care service, where we would await the death of the father, but in the delivery room of this new model of men and fathers who will revolutionize human relations.

Jesus showed us who the father is: He had all the authority to do it because He came from having been together with Him in heaven. He knew first-hand the provider, protector, sustainer, life source, the originator of a family or company of people animated by the same Spirit.

Paul is an example of how the revelation of the father can completely transform a man. In the first place, Paul was not rebellious to the vision of heaven that he received on the way to Damascus (See Acts 26:19) and through which he ended up becoming an apostle of Jesus Christ. Secondly, everything that Paul was and considered valuable before became rubbish in the face of the high value of knowing Christ (Philippians 3:8). He longed to win Christ, i.e., that the revelation of the father would take full control of his life. So it was that as the years passed, Paul became increasingly humble. Only a man who grows in humility considers himself the least of the apostles (See 1Corinthians 15: 9) and as the years go by as "the worst of all sinners" (See 1Timothy 1:15.) For Paul, this is not a formula, but a sincere opinion deep in his heart.

The church has not yet dimensioned the magnitude of the power and anointing that is hidden in the knowledge of the father.

In the past dispensations, the father hid from men. Only a few lucky ones could see any theophany of his presence. Moses, the greatest prophet, saw the backs of God.

Isaiah said: "I saw the Lord sitting on his throne". That is why the Bible says in (Hebrews 1.1) *"God having spoken to parents many times and in many ways through the prophets"*, in these last days he has spoken to us through the Son...

At the end times, we are now; there is a decline of the fatherhood function. Thus we assist a childish contemporary man, consumer compulsive of stimuli and pleasure, workaholic, a teenager who wants to be young eternally, who nevertheless refuses to bear the slightest fault or deprivation in other areas, which shows, as we will see later, precisely that absence of father.

There will come a day in your spiritual growth when you become a spiritual Father. A Father is one who is a mature believer who carries the presence of God within him. A Father is one who carries in himself the same genes as the one who procreated him; He will reproduce in the same kind of life that gave him life. He will bring to his offspring the very nature of the one who begot him.

A spiritual father is someone who cares for us, who conveys to us love, identity, spiritual covering, who prays for us and is concerned for our happiness. In return, we love, honor, serve, and care. We also give in return to make our spiritual fathers work easy and receive covering from them, and grace, and the blessing of Christ.

Absence of father, who, on the other hand, naturally hinders belief experience in a good and provident God the Father, a process accompanied by the same time for secularization promoted from philosophical, political, and even religious.

A Father in the Spirit reproduces the spiritual life. Jesus said, "*It is the spirit that gives life, the flesh does not profit at all: the words that I speak to you, they are spirit, and they are life*" (John 6:63). When we learn to speak from our Spirit the words of God, then our words also become Spirit and life we can impart life to others through our words.

As we have seen, in each reform that the Holy Spirit has brought into the church to advance God's purpose to a new phase, there have always been pioneers who were willing to pay the costs of the misunderstanding, discredit, and intolerance of their contemporaries, but these rose as spiritual fathers of the generations to come after them.

In today's Christianity, how many pastors, evangelists, missionaries, or leaders, in general, would honestly consider themselves "the worst of all sinners"? We do not know! It may be that many have a higher self-concept and feel confused at the bottom of their hearts just thinking about it. Others more daring, perhaps, would affirm it as a light way of simply seeking honor before men in the act of false humility. The truth is that being truly possessed in the heart by the same feeling of Paul is something that is demonstrated in acting before God and in dealing with others, both in the church and outside it.

On the other hand, Paul also shows himself to be virtuous in kindness by manifesting his sincere desire to be considered anathema out of love for his Israelite brothers and that they could achieve salvation in Christ (See Romans 9: 1-5.)

How many preachers today, unlike Paul, use human tactics to capture the attention of the church? Some make their knowledge shine using elaborate words or theological constructions. Many openly point out their ecclesiastical titles such as Pastor, bishop, evangelist, or apostle; others point to their academic degree of teacher or doctor. All of this without spiritual covering. What good is all that if there is no revelation of the spiritual father? Moreover, if there were a revelation of the fatherhood, preachers would not need to use human tactics.

Furthermore, it would not even occur to them, for the Spirit of God would teach the church directly. Paul being an eminence in his time, instructed at the feet of Gamaliel (See Acts 5:34), he was concerned not to attract the gaze of men to him, but that the faith of his brothers was founded on the power of God. What a beautiful example!

Yes, a spiritual father is more than necessary to be successful in the ministry of a believer to progress. The spiritual parents' responsibility is to watch over the souls of the spiritual children and to account for all this to the Lord. They will not be able to do it well if there are independence and a certain rebellion on the part of the flock. One can be in the church without submitting to the spiritual parents; then, we can solemnly say that they are not part of the congregation. They are only there of the present body, but their hearts are far away from there.

As believers, the Kingdom of God will be placed in our lives as we abandon all Spirit and attitude of independence and voluntarily submit to the authority of Christ.

It is necessary to eradicate the lack of identity when every believer committed to walking in the faith should begin to seek to transmit their knowledge and experiences to other new believers who need guidance. This book will focus on spotting the importance of the spiritual parents, the leitmotif of spiritual fatherhood as an evangelizing response for our time, in a purposeful and glowing way.

In the light of the Scriptures, what this concept of spiritual father means. What a spiritual father does with his child (ren), the character and principles of fatherhood, the spiritual authority in the church, and the connection to a spiritual father, the blessings when honoring spiritual fathers, the growth of a ministry is tied to your spiritual father. In this book, you will find values that will assist you in your relationship with your father, not only in the church but also in your business, community, and other institutions. Reading this book will help you understand the concept of fatherhood and the development of men and families' lives, both biological and spiritual. In conclusion, we will present the spiritual fatherhood lived in a brilliant example of the King Jesus ministry, with the Apostle Guillermo Maldonado, has been a blessing to my personal and spiritual life in which his qualities as a spiritual father inspired me. The experiences I have learned from him as Pastor have fueled my desire to write this book and to our most significant effort, sacrifice, is so that those who will read this book may be edified in the Word of God and learn to have their walk with God, to serve Him, reaching His calling and also being fruitful in every aspect of their life.

1

SPIRITUAL PATERNITY

In general, the concept that a person manages of his father, for better or for worse, will be the same concept that we will have towards God; hence it is not difficult for us to see God as God but as father. (Luke 11: 2) *And he said to them, when you pray, say, Our Father which art in heaven, hallowed be thy name. Thy kingdom come. Thy will be done, as in heaven, so in earth.* It is important to highlight that one of the first things that Jesus wanted us to see was God as father. When God places leaders or pastors at our side, they must be seen as parents, (2 Kings 2:12) *And Elisha saw it, and he cried, My father, my father, the chariot of Israel, and the horsemen thereof. And he saw him no more: and he took hold of his own clothes and rent them in two pieces.* In addition, you, as a leader, have to show yourself as a father what others see in you that the son will do what he sees the father doing. (John 5:19) Jesus answered then and said to them: *"Verily, verily, I say unto you, The Son can do nothing of himself, but what he seeth the Father do: for what things soever he doeth, these also doeth the Son likewise".*

CHARACTERISTICS OF A SPIRITUAL FATHER

It is not easy to find a good spiritual father. Before committing ourselves to any spiritual father, it is highly recommended to examine and search the person. Therefore, according to the Bible, we think it is essential to highlight some traits that define spiritual parents. On the other hand, qualities can only have been acquired having been a good spiritual son of another father, obeying him, and letting himself be accompanied.

Assuming with responsibility, this task demands the possession of certain distinctive characteristics in the person who commits himself, which, at the same time, become essential requirements for success in fulfilling the objective of paternity.

Being a spiritual father represents a privilege that the Lord grants to all those who commit themselves to his cause.

As Jesus did, we are called to share the good news of salvation with others and lovingly care for them. The Apostle Peter challenges us to always be prepared, to defend the hope that is in us. The word of God is the same yesterday, and today, and for centuries, but we must know how to locate it in the different contexts that we move. "*And to Him who is able to do all things much more abundantly than we ask or understand, according to the power that works in us, to him be glory in the church in Christ Jesus for all ages, forever and ever. Amen*" (Ephesians 3: 20-21).

I define spiritual father as knowing where God wants people to be and taking the initiative using his methods to get them there in full dependence on his power. The answer to the place where God wants people to be is in a spiritual condition and lifestyle that demonstrates the Glory of God and honors His name. Therefore, the goal of a spiritual father is for them to get to know God and glorify Him in everything they do. A spiritual father is not so much about directing you as it is about changing you. If we are the type of leaders that we should be, our goal will be to develop people rather than dictate plans. We can make people do what we want, but if their hearts do not change, we have not led them spiritually. We are not taking you where God wants you to be.

All have the responsibility of leadership in certain relationships. However, my interest in this book consists of the characteristics that a person must have to be a spiritual leader who excels both in the quality of his leadership and in the number of his followers.

Biblically a spiritual father is made up of an inner circle and an outer circle. The inner circle of spiritual leadership is the sequence of events in the human soul that must take place if someone is to reach the first base of spiritual leadership. These are the absolutely essential elements. These are things that every Christian will have to achieve to some degree, and when they have been obtained with high fervor and deep conviction, they will often direct you to a place of strong leadership. In the outer circle, there are qualities that characterize both spiritual and non-spiritual leaders. What I want to try in this essay is simply to explain and illustrate the qualities of the inner circle and those of the outer circle.

Everyone in the church has one or more spiritual gifts. Everyone must be involved in the ministry. Everyone should seek to lead others to the point at which they give glory to God through the way they think, act, and feel. However, some people who have been given personality qualities by God tend to equip them to be more capable leaders than others. Not all these characteristics are particularly Christian, but when the Holy Spirit fills each person's life, these qualities are transformed for God's purpose.

Assiduous

Spiritual leaders long to change, move, reach, grow, and lead a group or institution to new dimensions of ministry. You have the spirit of Paul, who said in Philippians 3:13, "*Brethren, I don't think I have already accomplished it myself. Rather, one thing I do: forgetting what lies behind and striving to achieve what lies ahead, I continue to move toward the goal to win the prize that God offers through his heavenly calling in Christ Jesus*". Leaders are always people with goals.

The story of God's redemption has not yet come to an end. The church is pierced with imperfections, and lost sheep are not yet in the fold; there are needs of all kinds that the world cannot satisfy, sin infects the saints. It is unthinkable that we are satisfied with things as they are in a fallen world and an imperfect church. Therefore, God has been pleased to incite a holy upheaval in some of his people. These people are very likely to become leaders.

Hopeful

Spiritual leaders are optimistic not because man is good but because God is in control. The leader must not allow his discontent to become grief. When you see the imperfections of the church, you should say next to the writer of (Hebrews 6: 9), "*As for you, dear brothers, although we express ourselves in this way, we are sure that the best is waiting for you, that is, what concerns the Salvation.*" The foundation of his life is (Romans 8:28), "*Now we know that God arranges all things for the good of those who love him, those who have been called according to his purpose.*" He reasons with Paul that, "*He who did not spare his own Son, but gave him up for us all, how can he not generously give us, together with him, all things?*" (Romans 8:32). Without this trust based on the goodness of God manifested in Jesus Christ the perseverance of the leader would falter and the people would not be inspired. Without optimism, this agitation turns into despair.

Powerful

The great quality that I want in my associates is intensity. (Romans 12: 8) says that if your gift is leadership, "do it diligently."(Romans 12:11) says, "*Never stop being diligent; rather, serve the Lord with the fervor that the Spirit gives.*"

Spiritual leaders must isolate themselves and reflect on what unspeakable and stupendous things they know about God. If their lives are just an endless yawn, then they are just blind. Leaders must give evidence to prove that matters of the spirit are intensely real. They cannot achieve that unless they themselves have intensity.

Determined

Jesus said in (Matthew 24:13), "*He who stands firm to the end will be saved.*" Paul said in Galatians 6: 9, "*Let us not grow weary in doing good.*" We live in an era in which immediate gratification is usually demanded. That means that very few people excel in the virtue of perseverance. Very few people follow the march or continue in the same ministry when they face any significant difficulty. However, vision without perseverance gives rise to fairy tales and no fruitful ministries. My dad once told me that the reason why he thought that many pastors failed to see revival in their churches is that they were leaving just before this took place. The long journey is hard but rewarding. The tree falls after an endless stream of tiny axes. The criticisms you encounter along your way will be erased into oblivion if you continue to do the Lord's will.

Philosopher

"*Be children about malice, but adults in your mind*" (1 Corinthians 14:20). It is not easy being a leader of people who surpass you in thought. A leader must be the type of person who, when faced with circumstances, meditates on them. He sits down with a pencil and paper and writes, creates, and orders his ideas. It tests everything and stands firm in what is good (See 1 Thessalonians 5:21). He is critical in the best sense of the word and capricious or indulged in any new trend. He considers everything and takes into account the pros and cons, always having a reasoned analysis of all the decisions he makes. Being careful and rigorous does not contradict the need to be dependent on prayer and divine revelation. The apostle Paul told Timothy in (2 Timothy 2: 7), "*Reflect on what I tell you, and the Lord will give you a greater understanding of all this.*" In other words, God's way of imparting awareness and vision is not to short-circuit the intellectual process.

Prepared and Active

A leader does not like fuss. He likes to know where and how things have quick access for use. His favorite figure is the line, not the circle. He complains in meetings that they do not progress from premise to conclusions but instead navigate endlessly in irrelevant circles. When something has to be done, he sets up a three-step plan and presents it. A leader seeks to connect the links that activate a board decision to bring it into implementation. It seeks to occupy your time completely and organizes your schedule to make optimal use of your time. Set aside blocks of time to focus on your most productive activities. Use the small moments in order not to waste them. (For example, what do you do while brushing your teeth? Could you put a magazine on the shelf and read an article at the same time?). A leader takes time to plan his days, weeks, months, and years. Even knowing that ultimately it will be God who directs his steps, he must be the one who plans his path. A leader is not a jellyfish that is carried away by the rocking of the waves but an immovable oyster. The leader is the sea dolphin capable of swimming with or against the current.

Coach

I am not surprised that some prominent pastors in the church are also men of significant impact as teachers. According to (1 Timothy 3: 2), anyone who aspires to the role of a bishop must be able to teach. What makes an outstanding teacher? I think that an excellent teacher has at least the following characteristics.

- A good teacher asks the most difficult questions, reasons the answers, and asks provocative questions to stimulate his students to think.
- A good teacher divides the topic to be taught into parts, is able to see how these parts work together, and discovers the total function of the topic.

- A good teacher anticipates the problems his students will face and motivates them to overcome without losing heart.
- A good teacher anticipates the objections of his students and prepares himself to have a correct and intelligent answer to each objection.
- A good teacher has the ability to see things from various points of view and learning styles and therefore is able to explain difficult things in clear terms that fit the student's perspective.
- A teacher is a concrete, not abstract, specific, not general, precise, not lazy, direct, not evasive.
- A good teacher always asks and tries to see how each discovery during the learning process shapes the whole of our system of ideas. Try to relate those discoveries to real-life and avoid boxing.

Enthusiast

Here I speak directly to men who are husbands and leaders. Paul said in (Ephesians 5:25), "*Husbands, love your wives!*" Love her! How does it benefit a man to gain countless followers and lose his wife? To what precisely have we led our people if they see that the ultimate goal is divorce? What we need today are leaders who are excellent lovers. We need leaders who recognize that they must take the day to spend it alone with their wives from time to time; leaders who do not fall into the habit of ridiculing and humiliating their wives, especially with contempt in public; leaders who speak highly of his wife in public and spontaneously flatter her in private; leaders who touch them tenderly on other occasions beyond intimate moments. One of the great temptations of a busy leader is to treat his wife as a sex object. This begins to manifest itself when the only occasions he kisses her with passion and treats her with tenderness is in order to seduce her and take her to bed. It is tragic when the wife becomes a mannequin for masturbation. Learn what her delights are and how to bring her to the pinnacle of orgasm. Talk to her and study her wishes. Look her in the eye when you speak to her. Put the newspaper aside and turn off the television. Open the doors for her in a gesture of courage.

Calm

One thing is certain: If you start leading others, you will be criticized. No one will be a meaningful spiritual leader if his goal is to please others and seek their approval. Paul says in (Galatians 1:10), "*For do I now persuade men, or God? or do I seek to please men? for if I yet pleased men, I should not be the servant of Christ.*" Spiritual leaders do not seek praise from men, and they seek to please God.

If criticism disables us, we will never be spiritual leaders. This does not mean that we should be the type of person who never feels hurt, but that we should not be annihilated by pain. We should be able to say with Paul in (2 Corinthians 4: 8-9), "*We are troubled in everything, but not despondent; perplexed, but not hopeless; persecuted, but not abandoned; downed, but not destroyed.*" *We will feel the criticism but we will not be incapacitated by it.* As Paul says in (2 Corinthians 4:16), *"Therefore we are not discouraged."* Leaders must be able to digest depression, as they will eat it in abundance. There will be many days when the temptation to give up is strong because of the lack of appreciation on the part of its people. Criticism is one of Satan's favorite weapons for trying to get leaders to throw in the towel.

Perspicacity

Jesus knew the hearts of men (See John 2:17) and motivated them to be perceptive in evaluating others (See Matthew 7:15). Leaders must know who is suitable for each type of job. Good leaders have a good nose. They can detect limpets promptly, people who hear regularly but never learn or change. They can detect potential even when they see it in a beginner. In short, they manage to hear the echoes of pride, hypocrisy, and worldliness. The spiritual leader conducts himself carefully in order to stay the course without leaning towards the dangers of rigidity or, on the contrary, betting on indifference.

Revitalized

We begin this theme with the quality of restlessness, and now we end it with the quality of rest. *"If the Lord does not build the house, in vain do the masons strive. If the Lord does not take care of the city, in vain do the guards stand guard. In vain do you get up early and go to bed very late, to eat a loaf of fatigue because*

God grants the dream to his loved ones. "(Psalm 127: 1, 2). *The spiritual leader knows that ultimately the productivity of his labors rests in the hands of God and that God can do more while he sleeps than he can do awake without God. He knows that Jesus told his angry disciples";* "Come with me alone to a quiet place and rest a little" (Mark 6:31). He knows that one of the Ten Commandments is "*Work six days, and do whatever you have to do with them, but the seventh day will be a Sabbath to honor the Lord your God.*" (Exodus 20: 9, 10). He is not so addicted to his work as to be unable to rest. He is a good steward of your life and health.

Visionary

According to (Joel 2:28) in the last days (in which we currently live), "*the elderly will have dreams, and the young will have visions.*" This is the positive counterpart to restlessness. We must not only be unhappy with the present but also dream about what the future may be. In (2 Kings 6: 15-17), Elisha and his servant were surrounded by the Syrians in the city of Dothan. When the servant sees this and groans in dismay, Elisha prays and says, "*Lord, open his eyes so that he can see.*" The Lord did so, and the servant saw that the hill was full of horses and chariots of fire around Elisha.

Leaders can see the power of God to overshadow future problems. This is a rare gift - Seeing the sovereign power of God in the midst of what appears to be overwhelming opposition. Most people are adept at seeing the problems and reasons for not proceeding with a project. Many pastors come to ruin hampered by boards of directors who think they have done good and done their job by blocking every idea he presents. That costs little. Hope and solutions are expensive. Entrepreneurship is currently in short supply. How much do we need people who are willing to spend five minutes a week dreaming about what could be? The text says that the elderly will have dreams. Every new church, agency, ministry, or effort is the result of someone with vision and a willingness to embrace the vision quickly and with certainty.

Persuasive

It is difficult to lead others if you cannot communicate your thoughts clearly and convincingly. Leaders like Paul seek to persuade and never restrain men. (See 2 Corinthians 5:11). Spiritual leaders monopolize followers not through vain speeches and empty words but through strong, clear, and convincing phrases. Like any good leader, the apostle Paul aimed to have clarity; in what he said. According to (Colossians 4: 4), he asked his people to pray for him, "*Pray that I will announce it clearly, how should I do it.*" It is surprising and unfortunate how many people today are unable to speak in complete sentences.

Animated

Loafers cannot be leaders. Spiritual fathers "take advantage of the time" (See Ephesians 5:16). They work when it is still daylight because they know the night is coming when no man will be able to work (See John 9: 4). They "*are not weary in doing good*" because they know that in due course, they will reap if they do not give up (Galatians 6: 9). They are "*firm and unshakable, always progressing in the Lord's work, aware that their work in the Lord is not in vain*"(1Corinthians 15:58). But they do not attribute this energy to their own strength nor do they boast in their efforts because they say with the Apostle Paul, "*I have worked with more tenacity than all of them, although not me but the grace of God that is with me*" (1st Corinthians 15: 10). And: "*To this end I work and fight strengthened by the power of Christ at work in me*" (Colossians 1:29).

On one occasion, someone said, tired men run the world. A leader must learn to live under pressure. None of us accomplishes much without having set goals, and goals always create a sense of pressure. A leader sees work pressures not as a curse but as glory. You do not want to waste your life on excessive leisure. He loves being productive, and he copes with the pressure without allowing it to become worrying by sticking to the promises of Matthew 11:27.

All genuine fatherhood begins in a certain way as the fruit of despair; the knowledge that we are helpless sinners in need of a great savior. This moves us to listen to God in his word and cry out for prayerful vision. This leads us to trust God and wait on his great and precious promises. This frees us in order to have a life of love in service that, in the end, makes people see and give glory to our father in heaven.

2

RESPONSIBILITY OF THE SPIRITUAL PARENTS

Our parental responsibility goes through different stages according to the growth of the children. In the first years of life, our involvement is decisive. Our prophetic commitment acquires a greater dimension at this stage: that of adequately representing God before our children as they grow; our task is to lead you to a more personal and direct relationship with God. The emphasis is on teaching them to relate to God and not to the Church; although one thing leads to another as they grow, priestly responsibility becomes more relevant.

PRIESTHOOD RESPONSIBILITY

The responsibility of the spiritual father is fundamental and complex. The task is also excellent, as it assumes that enormous inheritance, the image of unchanging faith, of strong hope and evangelical love, avoiding all the obstacles that might appear on his way when guiding his spiritual children, according to the will of God. By being ordained a spiritual father, the priest also receives the divine mandate that explains what his mission will be: "*Try to be the model of the believers for your way of speaking, your conduct, your charity, your faith, and your irreproachable life*" (I Timothy 4:12).

Nor is your spiritual children's responsibility easy because they will have to face many tasks, the most important being the freedom of their salvation. The path to redemption begins when you return to God with the feeling and awareness of your perdition. This awareness forces us to seek a Redeemer and makes many come closer to the Church. The first obstacle stone could appear for the individual who awakens to spiritual life and for the confessor who receives this "spiritual newborn", to educate him.

Parents, you have an eternal calling from which you will never be relieved: that of being parents. Calls in the Church are significant, but they are always given for a period, and then the person is relieved of them. On the contrary, the call to be parents is eternal, and its importance continues beyond this life. It is a call for this life and all eternity.

Parents are the figure of God in our home. Being a father and a mother is serious; more serious than being a good boss; more severe than being a good worker at the Church's service; more serious than being an excellent professional. After all, God will not hold us accountable for how good we were as workers and hold us responsible for the children He gave us.

The maturing of the father's faith and its influence on his children is one of the most fantastic means of grace. The father's faith will enter the family under the grace of God. Because of the parents' commitment to God, they commit themselves to their children.

PARENTAL RESPONSIBILITY IN THE OLD TESTAMENT

We see the example of Abraham and Isaac: (See Genesis 13:18, 26:25) before planting the tent and digging the wells, the first: They built the altar and called on the name of Jehovah. This is the father's first task: to build his house as an altar to God, wherein in all situations, the name of God is invoked. Our faith in God's promises reaches our children. In the Old Covenant, we see that promises were made to a person, and he accepted them for himself and for his children.

The purpose of the promise is to provide security and a warranty. These promises will come true by overcoming doubt, fear, and unbelief. We have potent promises that we can hold on to. The word says in (Genesis 17: 7) *And I will establish my covenant between me and you, and your descendants after you in their generations, by perpetual covenant, to be your God, and that of your descendants after you.*

The revelation given to each parent affects the entire family. At Easter, the father sprinkled the house with the blood of one lamb per family (See Exodus 12: 2, 7, 13). The blood will be a sign to them. The father sprayed the house as a demonstration of the desire for liberation for his home. He put a mark that differentiated him from the others. Through blood, he announced to the world and to the host his desire that his house be saved. Thus, the father ensures the children's spiritual protection; what makes him fit is his desire for liberation from the destruction of his children. There are potent promises that our children will achieve the same protection, freedom, and redemption.

The PARENTAL RESPONSIBILITY IN THE NEW TESTAMENT

In the New Covenant, the believing parent by faith appropriates the grace of God. Walking in intimacy with God ensures that grace flows over the entire family providing salvation for their children. (See Acts 2:39) is this promise to you and to your children? Otherwise, your children would be unclean, while they are now holy; we have to transmit this conviction to our children so that they can say: I am the Lord. Right away, we have the responsibilities that every spiritual father must have to raise healthy and mature children. (See 1 Corinthians 7:14.)

Love your children

Because being loved is one of the greatest needs that human beings experience. In the same way, spiritual parents should offer brotherly love to their children (See Philippians 1: 8). That love must transmit confidence to spiritual children to bravely face any adversity that arises against them.

Feed your kids

The father has prepared food; it is the table of the house. Although he has many food options, the son seeks to eat from the father's table. Because he knows his son's needs, the father knows what the food necessary for healthy growth is, what dose is appropriate, and when to give food to his son. This is part of parental care. Only real parents adequately feed their spiritual children. (See 1 Peter 2: 2.)

Support your children

Another task of parents is to serve as a support or spiritual, emotional support and even in other areas. An essential need of every child is to know that he has a father to whom he can go in time of need or anguish. The father becomes essential to support his children; just knowing him close in need is what the children are looking for.

Provide to your children

Even though the children have grown, they will continue to reach out to parents for support in times of need because they know that parents are a source of resources. A parent is a provider of material resources, but a spiritual father is a provider of spiritual resources. Spiritual parents can provide vision, anointing, direction, counsel, etc.

Replacement

A natural desire in parents is to reproduce in children. This means two things: that the children look like them, and at the same time, transmit to them what they have received from the Lord, prompting their children to go beyond where they have arrived. Parents want their children to be an extension of their ministry and have even more than they have. One way to multiply is to have many children who reproduce their anointing and calling. (See 2 Kings 2: 9.)

FATHERHOOD SPIRITUAL, A PLAN FOR THE GROWTH OF THE CHURCH

In a healthy church, numerical growth comes naturally. However, for the growth cycle to take its course, the Church must remain healthy. This can only be accomplished if we get each of the new believers to be cared for and cared for by another believer who is mature in God's way. The idea is that every leader or disciple who wins a person for Christ becomes a spiritual father or mother and can bring the new believer to maturity so that this new believer can finally fulfill God's purpose for your life.

When parents properly raise their children, they learn that, even if they fail or make mistakes, their parents will not reject them but will help and advise them to overcome their failures. This is due to parents' care and unconditional love and their desire to see their children developed, matured, and fully realized in life. That environment of unconditional care and love creates a safe place amid the child's turbulent world, where he loses his fear of talking about his problems and difficulties.

Lack of parents, either mom or dad, or both, creates insecure, immature, immoral, or troubled children in the absence of proper direction in their lives. The problem of our times is that the home and family are disintegrating, and many children lack moral character. Millions of children do not have a father who affirms and encourages them. Moreover, a lot of them do not even know who their father was.

The same thing happens in many congregations. They have so many integration problems that new believers do not have a spiritual father to take care of them and guide them. Someone won these new believers, someone fathered them in the Lord, but they were left to fend for themselves. Some of them manage to survive in the Church. However, with many difficulties, and although they tend to grow somehow, many of them become timid insecure believers, and in the worst case, rebellious and troublesome believers. That is why each person who is born again in the

Kingdom of God needs a spiritual father or mother, who loves him, cares for him, guides him, and directs him towards maturity on the path of God.

A spiritual father is one who invests his life, gifts, abilities, money, and resources to bring a child out of abandonment and lead him to spiritual growth. It also gives him an identity, elevates him, and leads him to find his purpose in God. He is the person that God uses as a source to provide us with the necessary resources to grow; teaches us the ways of God; He is the person that God uses to feed us and give continuous life to our spirit.

3

THE MODEL OF FATHERHOOD

We all want to be good parents, and we expect children to be obedient and follow the right standard in character and life. Being a father of God does not mean that we need to have perfect children. Well, God is perfect and has imperfect children like us.

Fatherhood is not the same as perfectionism. We want to be perfect and have excellence in everything we do, does not mean that our children will be 100% perfect.

Children must learn by making decisions and living the reality of their mistakes and failures, as well as their successes. Thus, they will see the qualities of character better in us as parents.

The Our Father Prayer is just one of the teachings that we can read in the Bible, and that expresses God's desire to be loved as a father. This divine longing can be observed throughout the Word of God, from Genesis to Revelation. In all things, we can see God revealing himself as a father. Therefore, based on the Holy Book's teachings, I want to talk about God's paternity and my model of paternity, which I believe corresponds to the divine. The essential identity that we can have of the Lord is that He is "Heavenly Father" and that we all aspire to meet with Him one day.

I can think of God as the best father because I have the privilege of having the best father in the world. And just as my father has exercised paternity by "adoption," when he welcomes spiritual children in different parts of the world, Heavenly Father has adopted us as children, loving us with all his heart.

As it is written in (Ephesians 1.5): "*And in his love, he predestined us to be adopted as children, through Jesus Christ, according to the benevolence of his will.*"

Jesus Christ is the only son of God. He has a full right to receive the Lord's fatherly love, but He allows us to be adopted through our faith. When the Lord, like the father who adopts a child, adopts us, we have all the rights that this paternity gives us.

I believe that my father exercises spiritual paternity, giving those who are received in his spiritual coverage the rights of a son, is paternity by adoption that generates in his heart a true love, the same love that he feels for his "children of blood." This spiritual parenting gives the same blessings that I have in your ministry to my foster brothers. This is the model of what God does. "*See how great the love that the father has given us: to be called children of God, what we are! That is why the world does not know us because it did not know it*", says the Bible in (1 John 3.1). God's great fatherly love, which reached us through Jesus Christ, gives us the right to be called children. As (John 1:12) says, "*However, to those who received him, to those who believed in his name, he gave them the right to become children of God.*" We are given the right to become children of God. This is tremendous! That is, whoever accepts Jesus Christ as a savior is adopted as a child of God. When we are adopted as a child, we become part of God's family and receive all the privileges of children, including His unconditional love. In addition, whoever receives spiritual adoption, being welcomed by the love of God, he begins to feel the fullness of divine love in his spirit. Because "*the Spirit himself testifies to our spirit that we are children of God*" (Romans 8.16).

Elisha as father

Let us look at what the Bible reports about fatherhood exercised through various characters in the Bible: Elijah's Fatherhood. Elijah assumed the spiritual fatherhood that God had given him: "*So Elijah went from there, and found Elisha, son of Shaphat, who was plowing with twelve oxen before him, and he was with the twelfth; and Elijah passed over him, and cast his cloak over him*" (1 Kings 19:19). Analyzing the text above, we see that Elisha was a successful man. He had twelve ox joints. Imagine that whoever had only one ox board was already considerably prosperous. Therefore, Elisha was a prosperous man, but that was not God's identity. The prophet Elijah, knowing this, went to Elisha and threw on his cloak, showing him the identity that God had given him. In another Biblical passage, we see that Elijah also proved to be a provider spiritual father for Elisha: "*It happened that when they had passed, Elijah said to Elisha, 'Ask me what you want me to do to you, before it is taken from you. And Elisha said, I ask that there be a double portion of your spirit upon me*" (2 Kings 2: 9). Elijah knowing of his role as a spiritual father to supply his "son" Elisha releases the anointing to him, providing the continuity of God's ministry. Note that he was not selfish; he did not retain God's legacy on his life, as he was aware that the work needed to continue.

"*And Elisha was sick from the disease that he died of, and Jehoash, king of Israel, came down to him, and wept on his face, and said, My father, my father, the chariot of Israel, and his horsemen!*" (2 Kings 13:14).

Most churches do not know for sure who their spiritual father is. They do not have a reference to a spiritual father. To have a spiritual father is to have someone who, by the grace of the Lord, is called to minister to the Church. The spiritual father draws on the Church's potential through apostolic anointing by training and assisting leadership in developing his calling. The apostle is someone who transfers spiritual wealth to the life of the leader. Let us check the text below and analyze it:

"He said, *'I am your father's God, the God of Abraham, the God of Isaac, and the God of Jacob. And Moses covered his face, because he was afraid to look at God.'* (Exodus 3: 6). We find in this text that God is a God of transference and generations! God himself presented himself to Moses as the God of generations. Your interest is to impact generations! He does not want to affect just one generation or a few people, but he wants to transform generations!

We observe that the Bible reports that in each generation God raised men with the function of fatherhood (Abraham, Moses, Joshua ...). Likewise, today, God raises up fatherhood for His Church by continuing healthy multiplication in his spiritual children. The church of Christ must recognize that it needs leaders who leave a legacy to their children and their children's children: "*The good man leaves an inheritance to his children's children, but the sinner's wealth is deposited for the righteous*" (Proverbs 13:22). Responsible and loving fatherhood declares the best about their children and generates a secure identity, without double spirits; that is, it causes an affirmative identity in Jesus.

Paul's Father Model

Paul shows us in (1 Thessalonians 2: 3-13) a model of a spiritual father. In his treatment, he is sincere and honest to win them for Christ. As you can see, we do not preach with deception or with impure intentions or tricks. For we speak as messengers approved by God, who were entrusted with the Good News. Our purpose is to please God, not people. Only he examines the intentions of our hearts. As you well know, not once did we try to win them by flattering them. In addition, God is our witness that we never appear to be friends with you in order to get money from you! As for human praise, we have never sought it from you or from anyone. Verses (3-6) Take care of new believers as a mother takes care of her children.

As apostles of Christ, we certainly had the right to make certain demands of them; however, we were like children among you. On the other hand, we were like a mother who feeds and cares for her children. We love you so much that we not only present the Good News of God to you, but we also open our own lives to you. It is an example for new believers. Do you not remember, dear brothers, how much we work among you? Day and night, we strive to earn a living, not to be a burden to any of you while preaching the Good News of God. You are our witnesses — like God — that we were consecrated, sincere, and blameless with all of you believers. (Verses 9-10), Paul exercised paternity towards Timothy: *"For whose reason I remind you to awaken the gift of God that exists in you by the laying on of my hands"* (II Timothy 1: 6). Paul reminded Timothy what path he had to follow. He showed his identity in the Kingdom of God by asking Timothy to awaken the gift of God that already existed in him.

We once again see Paul concerned about Timothy advising him not to fail: *"Do not despise the gift that is in you, which was given to you by prophecy, with the laying on of the hands of the presbytery"* (1 Timothy 4:14).

Abraham's fatherhood

Abraham was an excellent father; he offered security to his son when he needed it most. Imagine Abraham and Isaac walking to the sacrifice in which Isaac himself would be sacrificed. Father Abraham remained firm, confident, and, without losing faith in his faith, directs his son: "*Then Isaac spoke to Abraham his father, and said, My father! And he said: Here I am, my son! And he said: Here is the fire and the wood, but where is the lamb for the burnt offering? And Abraham said, God will provide you with the lamb for the burnt offering, my son. So they walked together*" (Genesis 22: 7, 8). It is not for nothing that Abraham is called the father of faith! They are a source of provision for the son's religious life and, as I say, "the father eats grass so that the son can feed on the milk that flows."

Moses' Fatherhood

Moses was also a model of fatherhood for us. He covered Joshua's life in prayer and counseling when he went to war. Moses blessed the life of his spiritual son:

"*And Joshua did as Moses told him, fighting against Amalek; but Moses, Aaron, and Hur went up to the top of the hill. And it so happened that when Moses raised his hand, Israel prevailed; but when he lowered his hand, Amalek prevailed. But Moses' hands were heavy, so they took a stone, and placed it under it, to sit on it; and Aaron and Hur held their hands, one on one side and the other on the other; so his hands remained steady until the sun went down. And so Joshua undid Amalek and his people, with the edge of the sword*" (Exodus 17:10).

In conclusion, parents support their children. A loving father raises his son's value when he treats him well when he politely ministers to his son by throwing prophetic blessings upon him. A father who praises, encourages, and corrects his son will make him a great champion!

However, as there are responsible and good parents, there are also parents who are negligent in their role. Parents who often do not offer economical, physical, and spiritual protection leaving their children at the mercy of adversity. For example, a father who treats his son with bad words may generate low self-esteem problems. This paternity does not follow the biblical model!

God has called us to a paternal responsibility. We have learned together with Paul that this must be part of our character, who has not heard the expression: "a shepherd has brought one more sheep for you to care for"; People have a distorted mentality about their responsibility within the Kingdom, not wanting to take responsibility for raising and caring for spiritual children, these people are living short of God's purpose, and we notice that people who act in this way are always spiritually ill, for of course sterility is the result of some pathological problem or even psychology, and this can apply within the realm. How many of us don't identify people who have had children change their behavior?

The same thing happens in our Christian life as we change our behavior. The lifestyle we acquire is differentiated because we have to be attentive to our children when they cry when they feel a stomachache, when they dirty their diapers, and when they start to laugh, to speak the first words, to take the first steps. Paul identified this in every life, in every Church he formed, he spared no effort, but applied his heart to instruct them, to help them, correcting them was always attentive, warning them of bad intentions. Paul was an example to his children.

4

FATHERHOOD AND SONSHIP

The sense of true fatherhood is, instead, and above all, in giving life. It means offering one space to the other to be himself at large. It is the sense of spiritual affiliation without which spiritual fatherhood and the free reception of himself as being-in-relationship. Regardless of gender and age, Father and Son, the physics of the people in question, are in the spiritual field metaphors that express a personal relationship. That is why tradition knows not only spiritual parents but spiritual mothers, too.

It is important to note that fatherhood transcends the biological. Affiliation can occur through adoption, making the person a father of your child even if the child is not your blood descendant.

Stages of growth of a spiritual child

When I was a child, I spoke as a child, I understood as a child, I thought as a child: but when I became a man, I put away childish things (1 Corinthians 13: 11).

The seed stage

This first stage covers from the first contact to integration into the cell. At this stage, the teaching for the new believer should be based on God's love; discussions such as idolatry should be avoided. Here you can use the "Follow Me" brochure to show you God's love and guide you to sincere repentance.

Childhood stage

This stage covers the moment he is taken to the cell goes until he is baptized in the Name of Jesus Christ. At this stage, the new believer should be given the preparation lessons to attend the discipleship class and should be introduced to the vision. At this stage, the first care is very important. It is the crucial stage because it is when the person decides whether to stay in the church.

Adolescence stage

This stage begins when the spiritual son is consolidated and ends. He is trained with the Bible about his new lifestyle, his relationship with the other members of God's family, and identifies God's purpose for his life. At this stage, the spiritual child needs to receive more solid teaching on the church's vision.

Youth stage

This stage of growth begins when the spiritual child is brought to the Maturation School. At this stage, he discovers God's purpose for his life, his Spiritual Gifts, and prepares to reproduce himself in others. The spiritual son is approaching the status of a mature man.

Adult stage

In this last stage, the new disciple is made aware of his need to reproduce in others and now be a spiritual father for the new generations. The disciple must receive adequate food to produce at this stage because this is the ultimate purpose of every new believer. Therefore, at this stage, you must start in the School of Ministries and enroll in one of them to serve others and thus fulfill God's purpose for your life.

The greatest delight of a spiritual father is to see his healthy children grow. This spiritual healing is the result of virtues that, throughout the process of spiritual growth of a child must be perfected and matured. Let us analyze each of these virtues:

The obedience

The prophet Samuel admonished his spiritual son, Saul,

saying: *"Does Jehovah take pleasure both in burnt offerings and victims, and in obeying Jehovah's words?" Certainly, obeying is better than sacrifices, and paying attention than the fatness of the rams, because rebellion is the sin of divination, and stubbornness is idolatry* "(1 Samuel 15: 22-23).

As a spiritual son, God rejected Saul because he did not learn the great lesson of life: Obeying God before everything. Spiritual children must begin, from the moment they are begotten, on an ascending level of obedience.

As spiritual parents, we should encourage our children to submit their will to God, to renounce their decision to do what seems good to them, and to submit to what God says in His Word.

Obey your spiritual father

Just as Scripture says that children must obey their earthly parents, so spiritual children must learn to obey those who told them about Christ. There will be times when the spiritual father needs to counsel and guide his spiritual son, and he needs to follow his father's advice in order for him to do well.

Obey the Pastor and his immediate leader

God has established pastors and leaders in his church to lead spiritual children on the path or process of spiritual growth (See Ephesians 4: 11-12). They are also the shepherds who watch over our souls as those who must give an account. (See Hebrews 13:17)

If a spiritual child is taught to obey God, it will be easy for him to obey his spiritual father and the Pastor, and his leader.

Respect

Spiritual parenting relationships require respect for the spiritual father. Respect includes:
- Honoring them in front of others by speaking well of them.
- Highlighting their virtues.
- Acknowledging their merits and experience.

This involves learning to listen to them and seek them to receive counsel from the Lord through them. Respect must come because of your work, your dedication, and your love for children. Respect is not required; it is earned.

Stewardship

Lastly, a spiritual father takes on the responsibility that his spiritual children learn to be good stewards of their time and money. Before being Christians, they were promoters of the kingdom of darkness because they lived in their means: drunkards, adulterers, cursing, etc. Somehow or other, with their finances, they supported the evil and corruption to spread. Now that they are children of God, they must learn to manage the time and money that God gives them, properly supporting their family and helping to extend the kingdom of God.

Essential Tasks of the Spiritual Father

Nevertheless, you know how Timothy has shown what he

is. Like a son with his father, he has served by my side in preaching the Good News. (See Philippians. 2:22.) The tasks that spiritual parents must perform for their children must be based on the love of God. Such studies should be aimed at building character and promoting the healthy growth of children. Here is a list of the essential tasks that every spiritual parent should do: Spending quality time with your children.

The true father genuinely enjoys spending time with his spiritual children; He invites them to his house, they go for a walk, shopping, etc. For the spiritual father, living with his son is a priority task.

- **Establish an educational plan for your child's development**

Every spiritual father must have a clear educational objective for his spiritual children. This plan must include the good news of salvation, biblical formation, doctrine, values, and spiritual habits and training so that he becomes, in turn, a spiritual father.

- **Form the character of the spiritual son**

The baby's character is formed in the first three to six years, and after this, only God can change it. Similarly, the spiritual child needs enough time for the relationship to deepen to such a degree that the father's love becomes a strong influence in his life. Children loved by their parents resist evil, both because of their conviction and thinking about the pain they would cause their parents if they went astray.

- **Establish rules and discipline**

The comprehensive upbringing of children necessarily requires discipline on the part of the spiritual parents. Discipline, in the sense of assigning them tasks according to their development capacity they have at the moment and practicing or being accountable for their task. But this disciplinary framework must be subject to an unconditional love relationship.

RECOMMENDATIONS FOR A SPIRITUAL FATHER

I am writing to Titus, my true son in the faith that we share. (See Titus 1:4.) It is very important that a spiritual father considers the following recommendations, which will help him bring his spiritual son to authentic maturity: A Spiritual Father must know the will of God for his children.

Moses knew God's plan for the people of Israel when they were brought out of the land of Egypt: Introduce them into the Land of the Promised. Although the people of Israel were rebellious in the middle of the desert, Moses, like their spiritual father, defended them before God. This Moses could do because he truly knew God's plans for his spiritual children. In the same way, spiritual parents have to know the will of God for their spiritual children.

A Spiritual Father must intercede

A fence is protection that soldiers put on to protect

themselves from enemy bullets when they are at war. Thus, as spiritual parents, we must stand as a fence against the enemy's attack against our children. That we spiritually defend our children to such an extent that we receive the attacks and not them. When a fence is broken, it is catastrophic. Therefore, the spiritual parents must be prepared to face the attacks of the enemy to defeat it.

A Spiritual Father does not neglect his responsibility

The spiritual father, under no circumstances, leaves his spiritual son. His love for him and his commitment to God do not allow him to abandon his son because he knows that this would mean possible spiritual death for his son, especially when that son is small in the kingdom of heaven.

The church needs men and women who have biblical knowledge and training capable of teaching others and people with the heart of spiritual fathers. These people with courage and dedication can lead others in the ways of the Lord and impart spiritual life.

5

LACK OF FATHERHOOD AND CRISIS OF SPIRITUAL DIRECTION

It is fundamental for the man who seeks God, from the beginning of his spiritual life, to know most safely his path, avoiding dangers and traps. To achieve this, he will find it essential to have an experienced guide that can help him with what he still lacks in discernment. This guide is what tradition calls the spiritual father and also a mentor. His role is not limited to teaching and direct, but accompanying, praying, and listening to God's seeker will help you get to communion with God.

THE SPIRITUAL FATHER IN THE MIND OF MAN

In the history of speculation, we find men who conducted a school of reflection and deepening and life, customs, spirituality, human perfection, inner peace, self-control, physical discipline, and morals. Classical antiquity has conveyed to us some names of these teachers, requested and desired by countless disciples, to whom they dedicated their lessons, and who have brought to us some works that enrich humanity's cultural heritage. We can quote Socrates, Plutarch, Epictetus, Seneca, Marcus Aurelius. All of them were looking for answers to the great questions that plague men of all times. They trained the disciples. They promoted the interior vision of the ultimate problems. According to the primitive schools' interpretation, they preceded and prepared in a sense the message of perfection of Christ. In their writings, they are seen as certain traces of the true divine wisdom and clear intuitions of the human longing for the one who would define himself the path of truth and truth itself: Christ.

In fact, their works are loaded with moral truths, precepts, and reflections, which are not merely the result of solitary thought, but the answer to other men's problems. As teachers, they can be configured with the traditional image of the spiritual father.

It is not excluded that Eastern Christianity was inspired, at least in part, by this typically human experience in concretizing individual relationships between a teacher who presents himself as an expert in the ways of the spirit and a disciple who is desirous or in need of this doctrinal richness.

The question arises whether the spiritual father must be a priest or not; what are the human and Christian gifts or qualities that he must possess: such as charity, discernment and discretion, patience and meekness, austerity, and the gift of the word; These requirements will subsequently give rise, with greater clarity and practical detail, to entire ascetic literature on the subject. Out of rejection, there is also the question of the need of the spiritual father, of the interpersonal relationship between the father and the disciple, of the disciple himself's duty to seek a spiritual father of fidelity, obedience, love, and respect. However, the Eastern Christianity offers a model of the spiritual father where the relationship between the subject and the spiritual father affects issues that touch penitential life, discernment of spirits, spiritual combat, and the aspiration to inner peace until union with God.

THE SPIRITUAL FATHER IN THE PAST

The first thing we discover is that God the father is the creator of everything, that he is the one who has been behind all creation, and that he is at the origin of everything because he is before everything. It appears in the book of Genesis and that, He is already there and that He is the creator of everything. He is the

THE REVELATION OF THE FATHERHOOD

founding principle of everything; He is the God of creation. He is the father god (origin of everything) and is, therefore, the source of everything; everything arises from him.

Since the first centuries, the hermits of the desert all have an Abba. They see him regularly and verbalize in front of him the "movements" of their soul to receive discernment and guidance. Is this necessary? It is useful for everyone, especially for those who want to follow Christ closely. It is fortunately traditional in the Church than preparing for holy orders or life nuns enjoy such help. It is almost essential; I think of the young people who seek to discern their vocation, to people who are going through great upheavals or crises, I am also thinking of people who live their faith in settings where they are not supported or are contested. I still believe in significantly injured or poorly balanced people.

The revelation of God as Father in the Old Testament is the first step to the Trinitarian mystery's revelation. From the beginning, we find the idea of God as a father, clothed in a completely general sense. Later its meaning is increasingly outlined as great divine paternity, which later, in the New Testament, is presented as a relation singular of God with his only begotten son. Thus, for example, they speak of Israel as the Son of Yahweh and God as the Chosen people's father. Yahweh remains Father of the chosen People too in the greatest afflictions and difficulties. The prophet Isaiah speaks of filial respect that the people owe to their Father God. In a particular sense, Yahweh is the father, and therefore the Book of Psalms especially encourages us to trust above all in God the Father. Finally, messianic prophecies call God Father for his unique relationship with the promised Messiah.

At the beginning of the Old Testament, in exodus, God, the father, defines His name, who he is, and does so with the revelation he has with Moses in the episode of Mount Horeb (attack of the burning bush). The name that God reveals I am who I am is what Yahweh is in Hebrew.

The name that God gives himself shows us that God is a mystery that we cannot limit. It is not something that we can say with a simple definition or with a name, but that God escapes human capacity, is more significant than human power, and exceeds human capacity. God is greater than what man imagines, and it is a part of the mystery. God has a piece of the puzzle. It also shows that God is not equal to anything that men have known and what is in the world. There will always be a dimension to know.

CRISIS OF THE SPIRITUAL FATHER

As we have been able to glimpse the historical profile that we have just drawn, the spiritual father is an unacceptable and hardly credible figure for men, even religious, in the contemporary world. Man has become more aware of himself, of his sufficiency, of his creative and decision-making powers. He needs a spirituality more incarnated, more attentive and oriented to value historical and concrete data, conceiving the Christian life more as an experience of faith than as a conceptualization of the revealed fact, more as attention to the word of God and man's response than as a reflection on it, more as prayer than as formulas of prayer.

Progress in our spiritual life, in other words, in our relationship with the Lord, is challenging when we stay only. That is why, from ancient times, "elder brothers" in the faith make themselves available of "younger" - obviously not a question of age - to help them on their journey. An accompanied person then tells us all the benefits that we can take away.

The spiritual father is called to promote a more personal and responsible faith with lively pastoral sensitivity, more mature and influential, as a witness to the gospel among the brothers.

LACK OF FATHERHOOD CREATES CHAOS AND CONFUSION

The spiritual father indeed occupies a place in the community and in the hearts of men who have chosen Christ. Still, he cannot escape a rethinking as required by the crisis in which the religious world and the ecclesial structure itself is being debated. It is in crisis, as has been said, not only the conception, but even the presence and acceptance of all kinds of authority, starting with family, school, social, political and, finally, also religious; it is understood, ordinarily, as interference in man's right to full freedom. Nevertheless, logically, it is a conception of the sense of liberty flawed at its root, since, to be authentic; the individual cannot reject the intervention of reason, the correlation of man with other men, the difference and variation of functions and services in the social and ecclesial body.

Spiritual father reminds us, aims to help the person accompanied in his "spiritual" life, his life with God, and reveal to him that the Lord loves him and that he loves the Lord, too. This second aspect is also important than the first, because sometimes the weight of sin – and guilt - may be such that the person judges himself and is tempted to despair of God and himself. There exists an essential difference between life moral and spiritual life. We can go through a period of ethical difficulties, to find oneself prisoner of bad habits, for example, and lead despite everything a spiritual life.

Therefore, the relationship with the Spiritual Father is not just any relationship where one is content to "discuss." It is a meeting where I put myself under the gaze of God to get to know myself better and thus be ever more faithful to Him, accepting on my part a genuine conversion to put Christ at the center of my existence. We can see that this relationship places us in what is most fundamental in our lives as men and as Christians, and therefore that we cannot stop at superficial chatter.

Crisis of fatherhood

Finding a spiritual mentor is sometimes more difficult than finding a life partner. For many people who have come to Church for the first time, the problem of such research is compounded by the lack of a clear idea of who and why they are looking. In the absence of spiritual experience, the newly converted Christian tries to be guided by the usual worldly stereotypes into a new system of relationships for him and, ultimately, is disappointed. A problem no less, if not a misfortune, is the lack of need for a constant spiritual mentor for a large number of parishioners who go to confession and receive regularly. It is not straightforward for a modern person to trust someone entirely. And without mutual trust, spiritual relationships are impossible.

It seems as if the image of the "father" in human relationships has been erased; even where a father exists and where he develops his paternal function, not only is the terminology avoided, but his activity is paralyzed or limited.

Spiritual father teaches us to discern the path and react so as not to be drawn into by illusions or evil spirits. He awakens and guides us like the action of a guardian angel. It allows us to take a step back from what crosses our mind and from everyday situations.

The spiritual father allows people to get to know themselves better, to put themselves under the gaze of God, to receive his peace; it helps to accept and live with the Lord the stages of our lives and to remain in communion with him. Little by little, we learn to welcome events, to discern, and to move forward, as we are, on the path of our life, each in our way.

6

UNDERSTANDING THE POWER BEHIND THE FATHERHOOD

It is evident that today a new dimension of the father figure is required, less authoritarian, but more authorized, less imposed, and more proposed, closer to the "model" than to the law. The discussion becomes more general and burning if we add the term "spiritual" to the name father.

A spiritual father is as necessary, relevant, and useful today as natural fatherhood (See Psalms 127: 4). As lack of a biological father causes tremendous effects in people's lives, so the lack of responsible spiritual fatherhood also causes many problems for the members of the body of Christ.

Can a pastor be independent and exercise his ministry without coverage? Many pastors ignore the importance of this topic and therefore do not consider it useful. When you obey your covering, you are obeying God. If you do not submit to your spiritual father, you also do not submit to God.

A father is also considered someone who not only puts the "seed" in the conception of the baby but is also in charge of its subsequent education and maintenance. If this is true in the natural realm, how much more so in the spiritual realm? Just as biological children, need a father to protect, instruct, provide for, and bless them; spiritual children also need protection, provision, and coverage.

Some church members are weak and stupid because they do not have a spiritual covering that guides them. If you are under spiritual authority, you are under the umbrella of God's protection and blessing.

IMAGE OF THE SPIRITUAL FATHER IN THE END TIMES

Given the many requirements to be an excellent spiritual parent, we could ask ourselves reasonably if someone would be prepared to be, much less, to consider ourselves ready for this ministry. The image of the spiritual father is received from God in large part for the good of the disciple's soul or the one who he comes to ask for a word of advice or relief. In principle, we can affirm with Paul that charity is the highest among all the charisms

(See 1 Corinthians 13). Not that excludes that some elders were hesitant to exercise the ministry for fear of possible temptations against humility. The solution gives it, how could it be otherwise, the obedience to the superior, or the consciousness of submitting to the will of God.

Therefore, far from selecting spiritual children, the spiritual father must embrace without discrimination against all who address him and employ his request more especially, according to the example of Christ, with the most disoriented, who are those who have the most need for guidance (See Matthew 9: 12).

Spiritual fatherhood today, even in the judgment of authorized persons, does not appear to be alienating to man's ability to choose freely and responsibly. Instead, it seems that it must be accepted as a human relationship, circumstantial dialogue, the experience of verification, and confrontation of Christian behavior.

A new era and a new terrain are opening for the spiritual father, both among consecrated persons and among the laity, in the sense that he presents himself as the "voice" of a new type of Church that seeks its identity in the contemporary world. He becomes an interpreter of a new kind of believer who accepts the gospel as a renewed and resumed personal option in each act and moment of life in faith.

Suppose it was necessary to summarize in brief words the most expressive aspects of a spiritual direction in tune with the times and with the men of today. In that case, it could be said that the spiritual father is the person who gives and awakens trust, who has understood the value of participation, which warns of the need to specify and point out the essentials of the problems. That stimulates the realization of God's plans without ignoring man's individual and social project, and that points out the path that through Christ leads to the father. He is and wants to be the image of this father, from whom all fatherhood in this world descends and comes.

A SPIRITUAL FATHER, UNIVERSAL FATHER

The entire project of the father is that the son lives. Dying is managing to give life. Today's father has to prepare his sons to be responsible and free men in a less and less cooperative society with the family, in a community with fewer and fewer parameters of appropriate behavior, virtues, and values. The family is not to manufacture soldiers, domesticated men, mere heirs, or consumers.

FATHERHOOD, AN EDUCATIVE VOCATION

In the specific action of the spiritual father, there is undoubtedly an attempt to accompany and sustain God's effort in a person to verify and validate it together with the person concerned in a typical effort to develop a secure Christian spirituality. This concern cannot separate from the effort to discover the divine project regarding the subject. The Holy Spirit's work brings it to completion. Its faithful correspondence to sanctifying grace; guides the person's perfection as an image of God, his morality in profession and vocation. The testimony of a Christian life lived with integrity; finally, by overcoming defects and weaknesses and giving rise to the acquisition of moral and spiritual qualities.

The Church has always recommended that Christians who wish to advance in their journey have recourse to a spiritual father. Since no one is a good judge of himself, God really uses this medium to guide and talk to you.

All ages can turn to a spiritual father, but it is perhaps especially in the maturity age that a spiritual guide's urgency is particularly revealed. At this age, the spiritual father will try to achieve orderly development and a mature vocational option with that freedom that Christ has given us; It will help make a synthesis of the diverse experiences and guide them towards human and Christian growth in the perspective of vocation.

The disciple is free to choose his spiritual father and abandon him if he does not help his human and spiritual growth. But such freedom should not encourage choosing a Father according to his own will, a Father who approves all his desires and does not teach to recognize and accomplish the will of the father who is in heaven. Obedience to the Abba is essential for the paternity-filiation relationship to bear fruit. The Desert Fathers used to say: "If you see a young man rising towards the sky by his own will, grab him by the foot and bring him down, for that is what is useful to him." This obedience aimed at the liberation of the self, of the will to save his life by oneself, because *"whoever wants to save his life will lose it, but whoever loses his life for my sake will save it"* (Luke 9:24).

THE SPIRITUAL FATHERHOOD BY CORRESPONDENCE

The most common method of the spiritual father is, without a doubt, the discussion, where the subject has the possibility of expressing himself and manifesting himself entirely, of returning to a topic, of being understood more fully, even in the details of a problem. But the experience, verified by people distinguished in science and the discernment of spirits, also admits spiritual father by correspondence when a personal encounter is difficult or when the subject feels freer and more secure by writing down his state of mind or difficulties.

The spiritual father by correspondence is one who invests his life, his gifts, abilities, and resources in visionary men and women who want to fulfill the will of God in their lives and have understood the principle of being under authority to have authority. To these, the spiritual father rescues them, heals them, gives them a name, courage, raises their self-esteem, and provides them with anointing, blessing, refuge, and rest. Furthermore, the spiritual father is a source of spiritual nourishment and revelation, nurtures character, provides parental protection, welcomes them into his home, adopts them as his children, and ultimately teaches and trains them to achieve their destiny and purpose in God. In addition, as happens in the natural, the spiritual father by correspondence applies discipline and holds his children accountable.

The spiritual father identifies the gifts and talents in his children and makes them bear fruit, unleashes them to their prophetic destiny, giving them direction and leading them to their purpose and destiny in God.

It is evident that the style has to be sober and discursive; the content should be about the essential, with the sense of moderation required to avoid incurring ineffective verbalism. In history, the letters related to spiritual guidance offer positive documentation, although this form should continue to be considered exceptional.

7

FATHERHOOD THE PLAN OF GROWTH

God's plan is that our children grow, mature in all areas of their lives, and one day they can form their own home, that every baby one day can have their babies. Moms or dads sometimes wish that our children did not grow up, that they stay five years old, at that beautiful age that they do everything to make us happy. However, imagine for a moment what would happen if our children did not grow up and did not pass that period.

THE PLAN OF GOD FOR THE SPIRITUAL SONS AND DAUGHTERS

God's plan is perfect, and so the challenge for us as parents is for our children to mature, to be raised in fear of the Lord so that one day they can form their own home. I see more and more young people who depend more and more on their parents. I know girls who are 23, 24 years old, and they tell me that when their husbands get married, they will suffer because they don't know how to cook. God's plan is that all babies grow, mature in all areas of their lives, and one day they can raise their children, children who are ultimately responsible. There comes a certain age in life when a son is responsible for his life, his finances.

God's plan is for every spiritual child to grow, mature, and in turn, bear spiritual children. Who is a spiritual baby? Scripture says that when you and I repent of our sins, acknowledge God, the creator of the universe, as our authority, and obey His words, then we are born into a new life.

THE PROCESS OF SPIRITUAL SONS

Jesus explained this to a Pharisee named Nicodemus in (John 3: 1-8) and said the following: *"There was a leader of the Jews named Nicodemus among the Pharisees. This went at night to visit Jesus. "Rabbi," he said, "we know that you are a teacher who has come from God because no one could make the signs that you do if God were not with him." "Truly I assure you, whoever is not born again cannot see the kingdom of God,"* said Jesus. - How can one be born again being old? Nicodemus asked. Can he enter his mother's womb a second time and be born again? "*I assure you that whoever is not born of water and the Spirit cannot enter the kingdom of God*," Jesus replied. What is born of the flesh is flesh; what is born of the Spirit is Spirit. Don't be surprised that he said, "They have to be born again." The wind blows where it wants, and you hear it whistle, although you don't know where it comes from and where it goes. The same is true of everyone born of the Spirit."

When you and I are converted, we are spiritual babies, and we must have a spiritual father who brings us to maturity. Paul spoke to Titus, his son in the faith and he said "to my true son in the faith," that is to say that he was his apprentice, to the point that he left him on an island called Crete, to put in order everything that was left to do. The instructions that he gives him verbally and that confirm him through Titus's book are to appoint elders, see that they were teaching the correct doctrine, put in order what remained to be done, and call attention to those who were teaching what should not be done.

THE NECESSITY OF A SPIRITUAL FATHER

Human being's most significant need is for a Father; men and women often cry out for a Father. Jesus Himself did not perform any miracles. He did not preach any messages until he received the blessing from his Heavenly Father. We read in (Luke 3:22), "*And the Holy Ghost descended in a bodily shape like a dove upon him, and a voice came from heaven, which said, Thou art my beloved Son; in thee I am well pleased."*

THE BLESSINGS OF A SPIRITUAL FATHER

God's original plan, and even today it remains the essence of his plan for the earth, is to bless the earth's families. He did not say that he would bless the earth's individuals, but he did bless the families. God's plan is to bless. The Devil's plan is to Curse families. When we talk about Blessing and Cursing, how does this, happen?

BLESS: God using humans to impart his message and image of Identity and Destiny to the heart of another human being.

CURSE: Satan using humans to impart his message and Image of Identity and Destiny to the heart of another human being.

Both messages are intended to affect the heart and are opposite of each other. God's message is full of Love, Courage, Respect, and Purpose. The Devil's message is full of Shame, Lack of Love, and Lack of Purpose.

Apparently, these phrases were customary for the Jewish Fathers to express and were common practice among them. The only person to whom these words could not be expressed was someone of questionable origin. Furthermore, since Joseph was not the biological father of Jesus, perhaps he could not pronounce this Blessing on HIM.

In Greek, the verb to BLESS (eulogeo), the literal translation of this word is "Speak well of (speak well of)" "It also means "Cause to prosper."

-The Parents, with their Words, their Attitudes, their Actions, possess the ability to BLESS or CURSE the life of their children.

-The parents have the nutrients that their children need to grow with their correct identity and blessed.

-But parents also have the Acid that corrodes the identity and destiny of their children, with their actions, their attitudes, and their words.

THE POWER IN FATHER'S BLESSING

It would have been impossible for a Jewish child not to have been given even one of these blessings. Their culture was shaped in such a way that blessing was constantly spoken to each other; that is why there was emotional, relational, financial health for all those who practiced blessing.

Isaac blesses Jacob and not Esau: (Genesis 27: 27-29). Isaac and his wife Rebecca and their children knew very well the paternal blessing's power on the firstborn; they knew the impact it would have on their life and their future.

Jacob was willing to lie for receiving God's Blessing. Esau knew very well that his full future was in the Words and hands of his Father.!

If we analyze the generations of Jacob and those of Esau, we note the following: Jacob his descendants multiplied in thousands, were healthy and had many assets, and did not experience plagues. Esau and his descendants did not prosper, hardly grew, did not get rich, and were often conquered by other tribes.

CREATING A FAMILY WITH THE BLESSING CULTURE

It is God's Purpose for children to grow up in a home with a culture of blessing. This is simply a home where members continually speak; pronounce the message of Identity and Destiny in God, where acceptance, identity, and unconditional love are shared. No one can do this 100% for our humanity, but we know how to recognize it and restore things to their original state if we make a mistake.

When the priest of the home gathers his family as often as possible, he must ensure that all the home members know and hear the message of the father's love in the particular forms of each person, without molds or models, in their own words.

HOW TO ESTABLISH A FAMILY BLESSING TIME

The father should look at each family member and ask if there was someone who felt hurt by word or deed, and forgiveness will be given to each one during the week. For this to be effective, no injuries of any kind may be left on anyone.

Begin to Bless each member of the family: (5 elements of a Blessing), appropriate touch, spoken word, add value to the blessed person, Paint the blessed future of the celebrated, and express the commitment to help all this be accomplished on your part.

Example of Blessings on Daughters

May the Lord bless and protect you; may the Lord always protect you against shame, May the Lord make you like Ruth and Esther. May you be worthy of honor from those around you. May God give you length of days, may the Lord grant you the words of this prayer, may the Lord make you a good wife and an excellent mother, may the Lord send you a husband according to the heart of God, and may He be your Provider and your Defender, that in all your ways your husband and children call you blessed, that God today and always gives you to eat of His joy and peace until the day you leave the land of the living.

Example of Blessings on Sons

May my God have made way for you in your walk, may the Lord rain down on you favor and grace before him and before men, may the Lord be your forehead and your rear guard, your shelter and your strength, may your hands be satisfied with abundance of the rivers of God, that riches and businesses are never strange to you, that the Lord will be the heavens over you from your youth, that the fear of God will always be on you from now on forever, That in your hands will multiply sprout and abundance, that your hands are always sufficient to provide for your wife and children, that the Lord make you a loving, tender husband, sensitive to her needs and at the same time that the Lord makes you an excellent father, a father that governs with the heart of God within you, that you are always a man of honor and of word, that your greatest wealth be always the fear of God and that your word be for others like fine gold that never loses its value, and may the Lord gives you joy in the midst of pain.

Example of Blessing on Wives

May the God of perfect love fill you with his love in and out, may all your dreams and deepest hopes be fulfilled, may your husband and children see you and call you highly favored, may the words of wisdom never be far from your lips, that your moves are those of a maiden before the Spirit of the Lord, that you are free to adore your God, that you never fear expressing your most excellent virtue, love for your children and for that man who fills you with happiness and of protection, may the Lord give you favor and virtue of being called before other "virtuous women."

May your heart always be protected from deception and mistreatment, may your virtue as the woman of God grow as the dawn of morning grows, may fear and shame never visit your dwelling, may her esteem never fall within your heart. May the love of your children make you feel satisfied, and may the love of your husband always make you feel complete, may the Lord multiply within you all the spiritual gifts that have been given to you, and may you hear in the night watches the voice of God giving you warning about your home, about dangers, that the Lord always makes you shine your age with all dignity and without wishing to change anything because you know that your inner beauty radiates so much that it spreads over your outer beauty, that you always find the time to give yourself love without feeling that you steal from yours, that the brave and warrior Spirit of Deborah is always in you, like the humility of Mary, that everything your fingers touch is filled with happiness and joy in God.

Some cultures are rich culturally, educationally, and economically because of the attachment to the traditions that made them strong and great. The Jewish culture was one, and it is one that promotes Integral Prosperity and not only partial. (3 John 1: 2 *"Beloved, I pray that you prosper in everything as well as your soul prospers and that you have good health."*

The key to comprehensive prosperity is to prosper in all areas and even the soul. A person who grows up with many wounds in his soul is a person who is destined for partial or no prosperity, so we parents must make sure that we are a blessing for our children and others.

The health of the soul is of utmost importance for every person, and that begins from childhood. A child, or a youth who is already beginning to show signs of the same sins and tendencies of the parents, is a child who is destined for partial failure or success.

Examples of blessings for spiritual sons

May God make you see the greatness of his creation; make you see how much he loves you and has been waiting for you to show you your destiny. May God be today and always your shield, your defense, your friend in times of difficulty, your best and only consolation, that at all times you have in your hand an offering to correspond to his care and mercy for you.

May the Holy Spirit break your limitation of mind, emotions, knowledge, and fears, may the Holy Spirit open you in all its wide-open extension) to his power and his wonders. That the signs and miracles are not for you other things but yours, your own, and you feel comfortable and calm to be an instrument in the hands of the living God.

May my God favor you with men, may the doors of employment open for you immediately when the time comes to have one. May material goods follow you wherever and whenever you are because you follow the giver of goods. Never put your heart or mind on riches, but rather that riches put their wings on you.

May my God put a woman for you according to his heart, which loves you, respects you, makes you feel the greatest in the world and has a heart that seeks God. May you have abundance in your descendants and that the good and happiness that you enjoy today are not comparable with the satisfaction that God will give you for being his son and putting your heart in him. If your father declares these blessings upon you with great expectation and Faith to believe that God will do so, receive the blessing, and wait for it to be yours.

Example of general blessings

May peace, tranquility, and happiness be your guardians every day of your life. Everything that your hand touches prospers, and that the rest of your days, everything you undertake your forces to do has a happy, correct ending and according to your wishes. You have never been the sandwich between your brothers; you have always been the balance between them. You will always be a source of compensation to all those around you and the rest of your life.

May my God open the deposits of abundance on you from your youth, and may you be an example to many men, both young and old, of what it is to be docile, humble, and diligent in everything you do.

May my God give you the family that far surpasses the family in which you grew up, in harmony, love, and prosperity. Kingdom health is upon you, and therefore, your children will also be healthy like the horses of Arabia. May your wife's love only encourage you to seek greater intimacy with the God who I believe you to be your heavenly father. My God place more sensitivity on you for the weak, for the needy, and for the one who has no father since you have had that kind of love in abundance. A new generation of ranges opens with you in the area of finance. God will give you the resources to pay your children's schools so that neither you nor they have to borrow. Your hands are anointed in the abundance of resources not only today but the rest of your days. Never allow jealousy or rivalry in your heart since you are unique in all your ways.

8

HOW TO HONOR SPIRITUAL PARENTS?

What is Honor?
    A -In Greek, it is the verb "timao," which means to have an attitude of honor towards someone; hold him in high esteem, consider him appreciated, with great value.

    B - Honor: Show respect, admiration, and esteem towards a person. Recognize or reward a person's moral qualities and dignity. Show respect for a person. Publicly show respect or admiration for someone.

    C- Demonstration of appreciation that is made to a person recognizing his virtue and his merit. Respect, distinguish, exalt, enhance, favor, prestige.

D-Honor expressed in words and without deeds is not honor. Honor is a voluntary choice that comes from the heart. If it is imposed, it is no honor either. In the New Testament, Paul commands us to honor ministries with money (1 Timothy 5.17)

HONOR SPIRITUAL FATHERS IS TO HONOR GOD

Many Christians neglect to respect and honor the servants of God present in their lives. Now the Word of God is very precise that we are blessed by God Himself when we respect our spiritual father because it is as if we did it to God in person. (Matthew 10: 40-42) *"He who receives you receives me, and he who receives me receives him who sent me." Whoever receives a prophet as a prophet will receive a prophet's reward, and whoever receives a just as a just will receive a righteous's reward. And whoever gives only one glass of cold water to one of these little ones because he is my disciple, I tell you the truth; he will not lose his reward. "*

Not long ago, I saw a documentary about a Buddhist country. It is enough for the monks to walk the city streets, for people to hurry to offer them offerings, be it money or food, in exchange for a simple blessing. When going to the market, devotees of a Muslim religion stood up with their urns, which many Muslims who did not even know them, in particular, found it normal to pour offerings into their urns.

Christians are the worst students to honor their spiritual

father and even vastly underestimate their role. Now it is to us that God gave this command and not to religion. The world steals and copies divine laws if we Christians are not the perfect example of Christ. How often our pastors, our spiritual elders, love us with the word that we hasten to get angry. How many Christians keep changing churches, or ministries, simply because the servant of God does his job by warning the faithful of his wrongdoing?

However, Jesus said that if we receive a servant of God as such, we are winners. This means that if we truly respect God's servants as such, our soul is blessed. And that if we respect them, we obey the will of God. We are going to see an example, which is David. He respected the man of God present in his life. Because of this, he found mercy before the Lord.

(2 Samuel 12: 7-10) *"And Nathan said to David, You are this man! Thus saith Jehovah, the God of Israel: I anointed you king over Israel, and I delivered you from the hand of Saul; I have put you in possession of your master's house, I have placed your master's wives in your womb, and I have given you the house of Israel and of Judah. And if it had been little, I would have added more. Why then did you despise the word of the Lord, doing that which was evil in his sight? You struck the sword Uriah, the Hittite; you took his wife to make her your wife, and he killed him with the sword of the children of Ammon. Now the sword will never go away from your house, because you despised me, and because you took Uriah's wife, the Hittite, to make her your wife. "*

David sinned before the Lord by committing adultery and

killing the husband of the woman in question. God sent Nathan to warn him and correct him of his sin. How did David react? He didn't insult Nathan, telling him to look elsewhere and not worry about what he's not looking at. On the contrary, he immediately understood that God sent his servant to put him back on the right track. Immediately afterward, he repented of his act, and God forgave him. We must never forget that our spiritual leaders are the instruments of God, sent to correct us, to put us back on the path of truth and justice. How many times our sins blind us, that we are unaware of our actions, that God is obliged to send these people to open our eyes. Whoever is faithful to his spiritual father, that is to say, to the person who puts him on the way to know Christ, that one will see himself grow spiritually and especially in humility. When he washed his disciples' feet, he told them that we have to do this to each other. Honoring the servants of God also allows us to learn to grow in humility. We will see a contrary example, Saul; his pride led to his loss.

(1 Samuel 13: 11-14) *"Samuel said, What have you done? Saul replied: When I saw that the people were dispersing far from me, that you were not arriving at the appointed time, and that the Philistines were assembled in Michmasch, I said to myself: The Philistines are going to descend against me in Gilgal, and I did not implore the Lord! It was then that I abused myself and offered the burnt offering. Samuel said to Saul, "You have been acting foolishly; you have not kept the commandment which the Lord your God gave you. The Lord would have established your kingdom*

over Israel forever; and now your reign will not last. The Lord has chosen a man after his own heart, and the Lord has chosen him to be the ruler of his people, because you have not kept what the Lord commanded you. "

Saul here allowed himself to judge Samuel, thinking that he was late and that by the eagerness of the people, he said to himself, that he could do well what Samuel did by offering the holocaust. After that, Saul's pride can still be seen by disobeying Samuel, and he disobeyed God. Therefore, his kingdom was taken away from him.

How often, in our thoughts, through our mouth, we allow ourselves to judge the servants of God; How many times do we criticize the preaching of our pastor, thinking that in their place, we could have done better. How often we whisper about how much our spiritual leaders lead the ministry of Christ. How many times they are angry when God sends them to correct us. Indeed, these people are the smallest in this world because they do a work of humility, a work of sacrifice to spread the Word of God. How many times these people endure the faithful's insults or how often they preach without anything in return coming from us Christians. However, there they are, by the love of Christ.

Let us remember from today that God wants us to look closely at these people. Whether in prayer or on a material level because he works for the kingdom of God. Their work is not easy; they face many difficulties and temptations. God wants us to pray for them, not to criticize them.

David grew up in the will of God because he respected Samuel and Nathan. Elisha received the double anointing from Elijah because he was faithful to him. Timothy was faithful to Paul that his name is registered among the epistles of the Bible. Therefore, we see how much respect for the servants of God is part of the Christian life. If we honor them, it is not to men that we submit, but it is to God because we obey his law. If we regard them as the instrument of God and not as simple men, we reap the heavenly fruits. Many Christians are not blessed in their lives because they overlook that they do not care about God's servants. Remember what God said to Abraham: I will bless those who bless you and curse those who curse you. Let us realize that the world needs these people to spread the Word of God. And if we love God, we want his kingdom to spread. Therefore, we will find it normal to support people in the service of the Lord. There are indeed Nathan, Samuel, and Paul sent by God in your life. Draw close to them and be a blessing to them, so God Himself will reward you.

WHY HONOR THE SPIRITUAL PARENTS?

Our spiritual father is one who invests his life, gifts, abilities, money, and resources to bring a child out of abandonment and lead him to spiritual growth.

A spiritual father also gives you identity, endorses you, and leads you to find his purpose in God. He is the person that God uses as a source to provide us with the necessary resources to grow. He is the one who continually teaches us the ways of God.

He is the person that God uses to feed us and give continuous life to our spirit. The honor of the father who expresses himself through natural resources is one of the factors that produce that the son receives the same blessing and anointing of the father (See Psalms 133.1-3).

We all have weaknesses, faults, inconstancies, and errors. God alone is a perfect parent. Even the best parents made mistakes and sinned. The Bible says, "We have all sinned." As a result, we are all perverted. None of us has perfect parents, and neither are you a perfect parent.

Many leaders or spiritual parents are unworthy of honor. They were abusive, manipulative, and careless. What is God asking me to do? Am I supposed to ignore the pain, show a happy face, and pretend that everything is going well? Not at all. But God is saying, and I want you to respect the position of the parents.

There are three sources of authority in life: the home, the church, and the government. Each of them has roles. They serve as the basis for an orderly society. God wants you to honor the position of parents (parenthood) regardless of the personality that embodies it.

HONOR AUTHORITY BEGINS AT HOME

It is a critical lesson that every child must learn. Honor the authority starts at home and helps determine the type of success we will have in life, in our careers, and our relationships. The growing child saying, "No one orders me!" will find it challenging to keep a job. On many occasions, you have to do what someone tells you to do, whether you like it or not. Therefore, God wants us to learn to honor authority. When you go to a judge and say, "Your Honor," you are not making a value judgment about this man's character.

Will my treatment of my parents affect any other relationship?

It is the main training factor in your life. Your relationship model is shaped at home. As an adult, even today, when you act in an incomprehensible way, you cannot explain your behavior because you are still reacting against your parents. Many marriages have been ruined because a spouse has never rehabilitated a relationship with a parent, and it externalizes their resentment on their husband or wife or their kids. He says things like, "You are just like my mother." Studies have shown that people who get along well with their parents have far less stress in their lives.

When to Honor my spiritual parents?

Honor is possible only when it comes from the heart. Honoring is not a matter of doing for doing, but something that comes from the heart.

Honor is not by imposition. Honor is not an option but an imposed heart condition. It is born by revelation.

He who does not honor is indebted but cannot be imposed, and the principle must be taught. If a leader does not value the word that his Shepherd brings, he does not honor God. Honor is when I sit at the feet of the master to listen.

How do I know that I honor the Man of God? When honor comes from the heart and decisions and actions are based on His Word.

As much money as you give your pastor as honor, you are dishonoring him if you take action above the word. (1 Timothy 5: 17-18) *Let the elders that rule well be counted worthy of double honour, especially they who labour in the word and doctrine. For the scripture saith, thou shalt not muzzle the ox that treadeth out the corn. And, The labourer is worthy of his reward.*

HOW SHOULD I HONOR MY SPIRITUAL PARENTS?

As a child, I honor my parents by obeying and respecting them. (Ephesians 6: 1) *"Children, obey your parents; that is what you should do because God has given them authority over you."*

Obey - do what they say, willingly, with pleasure, immediately. The Bible teaches that as long as you are under your parent's roof, you must obey them. Since you depend on your parents for food, clothing, shelter, security ... they have the right to plan your life. When you are self-employed, this is another problem. But as long as they take care of you and depend on them, the Bible says you must obey them. The same principle applies to your spiritual parents; as long as they spiritually feed you and they prepare you for everlasting life, you must abide by them.

As a disciple, I honor my parents by accepting and enjoying them. The older you get, the more you start to see your parents' faults. You begin to see their dropouts, flaws, cracks in the armor. It becomes crucial that you accept them despite their weaknesses.

Why should I choose to accept my spiritual parents? You say I had no choice. Neither do they both seem to be stuck. Therefore, acceptance is vital.

Acceptance does not mean pretending that they were perfect. It doesn't mean ignoring their mistakes. It is not to agree with all that they have made or to comply with all their requirements.

Acceptance means:

Acknowledge that God used them to teach you and to help you abide by Lord. Your biologicals, your spiritual parents may have been excellent, poor, or needy, but regardless of how they treated you, the fact is that they gave you something that no one else in the world could give you - they gave you.

1. Life... You owe them your life, regardless of how they assumed their role as parents. God chose to use them as your leader.

2. Listen to what they have to say. When you are self-employed, you are not bound by their advice, but you should not despise them. "*Listen to your father who gave you your life and do not despise your mother*" (Proverbs 23:22). You can disagree without being rude. You listen to them, grant them the kindness to listen to them, and you do not skip them. It is part of acceptance.

3. Acceptance includes forgiveness. The fact of life is that we hurt those we love most often - intentionally and

unintentionally. If you live together for any length of time, family members will injure you. Families must be built on forgiveness because we hurt each other.

Today it is not as popular to honor your parents as to lie on a couch and blame them for all your problems. (Proverbs. 20; 20)"*Whoso curseth his father or his mother, his lamp shall be put out in obscure darkness.*" Bitterness is self-destructive. It always hurts you more than the person you feel resentment for.

Even today, if you continue to hurt and be resentful and bitter about things your parents have done to you in the past, you are permitting them to control your life today. The "You make me sick."; you admit - "You give me back," You have control over me.

You must accept your spiritual parents, not despise them, listen to what they have to say, offer forgiveness. The point is, God gave you your parents for a purpose. Even those who have been severely abused growing up - does God want you to honor their sins, their weaknesses, and the wrongs they have done to you? No. But He is saying accept the fact that God chose them to give birth to you. God gave you your parents for a purpose, and he can even take this evil, transform it, and extract good from it if you choose to respond appropriately.

You honor your parents when you forgive them for what they have done wrong, and you choose to focus on what they have done well. (Deuteronomy 26:11) *"Be thankful for the good things the Lord has given to you and your family."* God says I must not only accept my parents, for good and bad, but I must appreciate them. It is easy to take parents for granted. Some of you have great parents, and you can easily appreciate them. For others, it is a little bit more complicated. I would suggest that there are at least two things you could appreciate about your parents regardless of what they were:

- Honor and value your spiritual father (Exodus 20:12, Deuteronomy 5:16, Ephesians 6: 2). It implies:
- Hold him in high esteem, consider him precious and of great value. At no time do you belittle, mock, criticize, judge, or gossip about him. Even when you know that he is imperfect and he experiences those imperfections, more than human weaknesses, you value what God has put in him.

You admire your spiritual father, not for human things, but for what he has achieved spiritually, and you want to emulate and improve him in his activity towards God. You "endorse" your spiritual father, you recognize, respect, and appreciate him for the gifts, anointing, calling, and authority God has placed over him.

Even when everything you hear from your spiritual father is scrutinized through the Word of God, retaining the good and rejecting the bad, you always maintain a correct, attentive, respectful, eager, yearning attitude of receiving and hearing his teachings for what that they mean for your maturity and spiritual growth in the call that God has made to your life.

You serve him at all times (See Josuah 1: 1, 1 Kings 19:21), in all areas of his life, in all the needs that your spiritual father experiences, including material ones, when necessary. You spare no effort to make the most favorable circumstances for the exercise of his ministry so that he can dedicate himself to the word and prayer (See Acts 6: 4). He is a spiritual squire in the broadest sense of the word, helping him in everything that is required, without limitations.

You are a companion for your spiritual father; you accompany him whenever possible, to serve him, care for him, sustain him, support him, in whatever is necessary (See 2 Kings 2:2, 4, 6), and have communion with him so that he is not alone (See 2 Kings 2:11). You give yourself entirely, in fulfillment of the vision that your spiritual father has received (See Habacuc 2: 2-4).

1. You can appreciate their effort

Being a parent is hard work that requires time, which sucks energies. As a biological father, I have a new interpretation of what my parents have endured. It's incredibly grueling to raise your kids. Have you ever considered how much easier your parents' life would have been if they hadn't had you? It is said that one can see the effort of a tree through the ages if one cuts it and examines its rings. Some rings are tiny; they symbolize the years of crisis and effort. I would say that for many of us, our growing lives could be enjoyed in our parents' gray hair. When was the last time you thanked your parents just for raising you? Who else would have done it?

2. You can appreciate their sacrifice

The burden of fatherhood is heavy. Only economics falters

today. If you are a parent today, it will cost you about a quarter of a million dollars to raise a child to maturity. Someone said that a father is someone who takes pictures where he once took the money.

When a couple chooses to have kids, they decide to give up other things. So, we should appreciate the sacrifice. What acquisitions would your parents have made if they hadn't spent that money on you, on your clothes, on your school, on your doctor's bills? (Prov. 23:22) *"When your mother is old, show her your affection."* (By the way, there are four stages in the life of a man: he believes in Santa Claus, he does not believe in Santa Claus, he is Santa Claus, he looks like Santa Claus. Enjoy it in each of the four steps.) It is a great transition when your parents become your friends.

A word to spiritual parents: If you want to be honored, you must be honorable. "Do not persist in scolding and harassing your children, making them sad and resentful. Rather educate them with a discipline of love." Paul says, do not panic your kids by being rude. Do not try to make your child your lining. "Educate them with kind discipline." Each child must learn two things:

1. Disobedience brings pain. Each person must understand this. God says that - you disobey God; there is a pain in your life. Each child must learn that disobedience brings pain.

2. Obedience brings freedom. You are trusted more, and you are more responsible.

As a spiritual father, the number one goal in your life should be to make sure your spiritual children are rightly trained in the truth and in the words of God. I want you to know that I held my breath for good when I educated my biological children and led them to give their lives to Jesus Christ freely. I know that if I die today, I will see them again in heaven because they all know Christ. I did not feel calm until I made sure my whole family was on the path and had made this personal commitment to Christ. I prayed, worked, and did everything I could to win this fight.

For some of you, this is a painful message. It is easy to honor your father and mother when they are reasonable, pious people. But some of you have pastors who have hurt them deeply. Your life has been devastated by this. I want you to know that the Bible says that there is a harsh judgment for violating children's rights, and the mistreatment and neglect and molestation and many other things - harsh judgment. Jesus said, "Whoever offends one of these little children, it would be better for him if he had a millstone tied around his neck and thrown to the bottom of the ocean." It is a serious matter. So, what does God expect from me? How do I honor a spiritual parent who has dishonored me?

God does not ask you to congratulate yourself. He is not asking you to deny the pain. He is not asking you to suppress it or ask for an apology for your parents, for their alcoholism, or anything else. God doesn't want you to hide it. He wants you to face the situation. It's difficult. However, this is the only way to ease your pain.

The truth is that many of you have pending business with your parents. Just thinking about it can make you cry and hurt your heart. Where in the world can I find a solution to this? You continue to react to your parents. Chances are that this anger will affect your husband, wife, your kids, or your friends because you never resolved it with them.

If you are still angry at a parent years later, you are always giving them a chance to take control of your life. It takes a courageous decision to make peace with your parents, but you have to release that anger. Admit it. Don't hide it. This may need to be discussed. It's a courageous decision to stop blaming and start being honest. What many of you have to do is pray to have an interview with your parents. Sit down and say, "Mom, dad (or both), I want to be free to honor the good that there has been in your life, but I can only do that if we talk about the pain, I have felt and that I still feel and come to a kind of repair of this pain. I want to forget it, go on with life, and forge a new relationship with my parents. "Face the problem. It is difficult, but you cannot continue your life if you do not solve it. If there are twisted things to straighten out, do it while it's time to try some reconciliation.

I would encourage you to share your pain with spiritual parents or mentors to get at least partial relief. But for your own sake and for the sake of your kids, stop the deception spiral. Stop it right away. God alone knows the pain you endure. But He knows, and He worries, and He can help you overcome this pain. He can even extract good from it if you let Him do it.

The Bible says that the church is a family. It will last much longer than your physical family. In terms of eternity, this is far more important. There will be no physical family in heaven, but there will be the family of God. Those of us who belong to the family of God, the church, will be together forever. Its duration will be far beyond that of your physical family. The church is a family. Become a member of local church, you will have lots of brothers and sisters in Christ, aunts, and uncles, and spiritual mothers and fathers. You can be part of a family that will never divide because it will be united for eternity. Find security, stability, and comfort and take care of relationships in the body of Christ, the family of God.

Begin today to Honor your father, God the Father, and your spiritual father (your man of God). Ask the Holy Spirit to reveal the powerful principle to you that will bring significant benefits to your life and that of your descendants. Remember: God honors those who honor him.

This has been a painful message for some of you. God sees and understands your pain. I invite you to ask God to help you. In your heart, say:

"God, help me to take away the pain and bitterness. Help me to forgive. Help me to start accepting, appreciating, and loving the good sides of my parents. Help me to forge a new, positive relationship, if possible. I want to be part of your family. Thank you, Heavenly Father, for loving me without reservation, and you made me for a purpose, and you will never abandon me. You accepted me, today I accept you, and I accept Your Son Jesus Christ in my life. I want to be part of your family for eternity."

9

MENTOR AND SPIRITUAL FATHER

To have a good spiritual father or mentor in your life is truly a gift from God. Your response to that gift will determine much of what happens in your future. Scripture says, "*Let the elders that rule well be counted worthy of double honor, especially they who labor in the word and doctrine*"(1 Timothy 5:17).

We inquire to know which person around us could be our mentor. The mentor must be available, and he must be known through various channels, whether by conversations or by references. The mentor must be little trained, has some experience, that he has even - the priest or the laity who accompanies - spiritual life and, typically, that it is itself accompanied spiritually to have an absolute assurance and otherness in the mission it develops.

You have to discover a person who is not perfect, but a believer: healthy and holy.

The mentor is a gift from heaven

Profound indications can shed light on the right person for our life. A mentor may refuse to accompany a person if he does not feel capable of it, or no longer has the strength or the time, or else experiences relationship difficulties with this person. There is an incompatibility between certain functions (superiors, bishops) and missions in the Church and accompaniment. Besides, a person can hardly give all their time to support, especially a spiritual father.

Mission of a mentor

It's a great mission for which we lack many guides. More leaders should be trained for this purpose, first, by living and knowing the word of God. One of the mentor's great qualities is discretion: he is called upon to scrupulously respect the secret of confidentiality and accompaniment.

These people must have acquired a good knowledge of the Bible, have a regular and firm prayer life. They must also feel that they have been sent on a mission to their brothers. You have to be in touch with the Church. It is not essential to be a great intellectual or to have an excellent knowledge of the spiritual tradition.

The seal of the Holy Spirit marks everything: the mentor acts in God or with God. He always fades, like John the Baptist, before the presence of Jesus and his Spirit. Thus, we are called to recognize God's action in others and take an act of trust in this action and our brothers. Its action passes through the exercise of the theological virtues: hope in the face of weaknesses, sins, the contradictions of a personal life. God is always greater than what we see. Charity welcomes the other like Jesus and loves him, as he is patience, benevolence, listening weave the garment of charity. Faith is the essential axis of what we live because we try to see the invisible with the very eyes of God: we look and act through him, with him, and in him.

MENTOR QUALITIES

- Seeks to give and invest in the development of some people
- Is willing to facilitate the growth of others through this process
- He is an apprentice colleague who seeks to be formed to lead like Jesus and in developing leaders.

Caring for one's spiritual life

Jesus affirmed that no disciple is more than his teacher is. These words of the Master par excellence refer to the fact that no one can make a person under his care and guidance go beyond the point where he has reached. We cannot talk about what we do not live. We cannot give what we don't' have. We cannot lead on paths that we do not know. Therefore, the mentor has a responsibility to take care of his personal life. How?

Pray

The mentor must cultivate the habit of prayer. This should be a practice that includes the various kinds of prayer: adoration, confession, intercession, and gratitude. He should pray for himself and regularly and systematically for the young man in his charge.

Teach the word

The mentor must teach the person who is spiritually accompanying the principles of God's word in a systematic and continuous way. If formal teaching occurs in the small group context, the mentor can take advantage of personal time to continue addressing the issues considered there, especially as they apply to the young person's everyday life.

A mentor is one who: "Cares for, guides and accompanies the mentor and grows together with him." It deals with the person to mentor, guiding him, accompanying him, and causing the necessary growth; it does so by active listening. The mentor listens carefully to his disciple to try to understand the individual's problems.

With his accumulated experience, he stimulates the mentor's learning through a mixture of questions and dialogue, without pressure and proselytizing of any kind.

Empathize with the mentor in a genuine, not feigned way. It offers advice, counseling, and motivation depending on the situations the mentor is experiencing.

At times in our lives, we sometimes feel the need for a mentor. Support is sometimes made more concrete before making big decisions in your life. It is often necessary to experience things one does not understand, which one does not know whether they come from God

The dangers the mentor faces

The mentoring job of a young person is not without its dangers. There are certain situations that we must know to avoid. However, if they do occur, we must know how to deal with them.

Spiritual mentor teaches us to discern the path and react so as not to be carried away by illusions or evil spirits. He awakens and guides us like the action of a guardian angel. It allows us to take a step back from what crosses our minds and from everyday situations.

Discerning what comes from the Holy Spirit or from us, *"The wind blows where it wants, and you hear the noise; but you don't know where it comes from or where it goes. So, it is with every man who is born of the Spirit "*(John 3, 8). The Holy Spirit is the source of the unexpected, of surprise: it sounds like a call. It manifests in joy to welcome, joy for which we were not prepared: a phone call or a meeting challenges us and surprises us.

We believe that God raises us and suggests such a thought: it will undoubtedly be bad for us in the medium and long term. To make this type of discernment takes time: the accompaniment is instrumental and decisive in these cases because we take the time for a conversation or to discuss several times on the same subject in a context where otherness plays its role. You can see better "before, during, and after" a decision. The time factor in the analysis of the origin of thoughts is essential. Mutual trust in this type of research is rooted in the conviction that the Holy Spirit works and is present in the mentor's hearts. He teaches us to say "yes" like Mary. When we trust, we take an act of faith.

Spiritual mentor allows people to get to know each other better, pose under the regard of God, and receive his peace; it helps to accept and live with the Lord the stages of our life and stay in communion with him.

Follow Christ and not my mentor

Take the example of Saint John the Baptist. He offers us a trait of what accompaniment is by stepping aside before Jesus and saying, "Behold the Lamb of God." He points to his disciples, and he fades away. In any support, you have to trust. This confidence increases as the mentor fades away, like John the Baptist, from our friendship with Christ. The criterion of good support is not merely to obey what I am told: this is not enough. Follow what the accompanist tells us about our own life because he refocuses us on Christ and makes us grow as a disciple of the Savior. This humility of the guide helps us to purify the relationship of any ambiguity.

The goal is to follow and imitate Christ rather than our mentor. So much the better if he is holy to us and gives a beautiful testimony. But let's look more in-depth than a simple imitation of his life. Let us always focus on Christ, whom he indicates to us. Therefore, we are Disciples of Christ in married life, in the business world, in studies. We are disciples of Christ and not of a tremendous charismatic or intellectual personality. If we are single, it is not a question of becoming a priest like our guide. In short, we should not copy our life to his, but through his life and he is listening, "live our life" and offer it to Christ as we are. Avoid some improper imitation processes.

Examples of mentor in Bible

The Old Testament has a lot to say about mentorship. We see an example in Jethro, the father-in-law of Moses also called Reuel ("friend of God"). In (Exodus 18: 1–24), we find the friend of God serving in vital ways the leader of God as mentor and coach. Jethro advised and trained Moses when he went to meet him (v. 7). He took time to find out how he was personally (v. 7). He listened to what he told her about the ups and downs of his journey (v. 8). He was pleased with him (v. 9). He offered sacrifices with him (v. 12). He ate with him (v. 12). He observed his work (v. 14). He asked him awkward questions (v. 14). He made him see that he was not doing his job well (v. 17). He gave wise counsel (v. 18–23). Jethro is an Old Testament example of what a coach and mentor is. With great wisdom, he extracted what God was doing in Moses's life and at the exact moment deposited it to help Moses develop a plan to properly lead God's people. He was a friend of God and a friend of the leader of God.

Apostle Paul, a mentor

In (Ephesians 4: 11-12), the apostle Paul gave an order: *"And he himself constituted some, apostles; to others, prophets; to others, evangelists; to others, pastors and teachers, in order to perfect the saints for the work of the ministry, for the edification of the body of Christ."*

The Greek word Katartismos, translated as "perfect" in other versions, is translated as "prepare" or "equip." Katartismos is one of the best words in the New Testament to describe mentorship in part strengthening, restoring, and inspiring which contributes to building the body of Christ. Mentorship is an essential form of Katartismos to leaders. Coaches help leaders fulfill God's purposes in their lives and to make their contribution to the Kingdom.

Above all mentors, Jesus is supreme. His relationship with others — especially with his disciples, indicates many attitudes and activities to assimilate in training. The life of Christ is an inexhaustible source of wisdom and knowledge about how to train. He sent His Spirit to empower us so that we live and minister as He did.

You not only have natural fathers, but you have spiritual fathers. A spiritual father is that person God puts in your life to help you become all that God has called you to be. Spiritual fathers transfer a wealth of knowledge to their sons and daughters through the spirit of wisdom. Scripture says, *"He that walketh with wise men shall be wise: but a companion of fools shall be destroyed"* (Proverbs 13:20). To have a spiritual father in your life is a gift from God. Your response to that gift will determine much of what happens in your future.

10

THE NECESSITY FOR A CHURCH TO BE UNDER A SPIRITUAL COVERING

Can a pastor be independent and exercise his ministry without coverage? Many pastors ignore the importance of this topic and therefore do not consider it useful.

Man, especially at the beginning of the spiritual path, experiences manifests a specific resistance to putting oneself in the hands of a spiritual father, to let himself be guided and cured by him, mainly because this requires him, as we will see then reveal your inner life to him and show him your problems. We must recognize that it is not easy to find a good spiritual father. Before committing ourselves to a spiritual father, it is highly recommended to examine and scrutinize the person.

"*Luke 7: 8: For I also am a man set under authority, having under me soldiers, and I say unto one, Go, and he goeth; and to another, Come, and he cometh; and to my servant, Do this, and he doeth it.*"

No person in the church can be independent of a delegated authority. To be in God's order, you need to have a delegated authority over it. Even Jesus is subject to a spiritual authority or spiritual father (John the Baptist).

In recent years, God has been restoring the apostolic in the church. The apostolic does not consist only in recognition of apostolic ministries, but even more, in the restoration of paternal character and authority in the church,

A ministry where spiritual fatherhood is not recognized produces servants, but no children, and therefore is out of God's order because the church is a church of children (See John 1:12).

Servants do not receive the inheritance, only children (therefore, Abraham urged God to give him a son so that he would not have to inherit a servant.).

Elijah inherited the double anointing from Elisha who said of Elijah: My father, my father!

Gehazi did not receive Elisha's double anointing because he was not a son but a servant, and Elijah took the inheritance to the grave (the anointing of his bones raised a dead man).

In many ministries, when the leader dies, even if they are successful ministries, the ministry ends because he had no spiritual children to pass on the inheritance, only servants.

DEFINITION OF SPIRITUAL COVERAGE

Coverage means to protect and safeguard, and today those who protect are the congregants to their leaders instead of the leaders to their congregants. When I speak of covering, I am not talking only in the spiritual sense but in the physical, soul, and mind.

Nowadays, what we see in the churches is that when someone has a problem, the only thing they do is pray for him, as if their leaders were spiritual people and a spiritual person is the one who solves the problems of his physical, spiritual, etc., and he does not wash his hands like Pilate and reduces everything to prayer. A leader who forces, intimidates, or persuades his members to remain under his cover, is acting in a sectarian and controlling way as in a dictatorship because the Christian must not be under the control of anyone, because he is free since Christ freed him.

In the pages that follow, I try to make my way through the vapor surrounding the difficult issues tied to the doctrine of "coverage," such as leadership, authority, and legal responsibility. Additionally, I seek to draw the general lines of an integral model that allows us to understand how genuine spiritual authority operates in the ekklesía (church).

Not all of these definitions are adequate to speak of spiritual coverage, but analyzing all of them, we can summarize that Spiritual coverage is: "the act of covering (protecting) a pastor with authority backed by God, to give him legitimate support and authority over others. At the same time that it is under the authority of someone higher up, and that this authority, in turn, comes from God".

Church with God's coverage is the one that directs the church subject to the theocracy of Christ, guided by the Holy Spirit and directed under biblical patterns (texts under their contexts). A church without God's coverage is the one that has extracted from the Bible many verses out of context to lead the church, preaching of Jesus Christ, and are sometimes guided by the grieving Holy Spirit.

Being under a spiritual coverage means, first, to live a covenant relationship. The first step in living a process of spiritual coverage is to establish an alliance with the leader who will cover us. Covenant is more than a commitment; it is a pact celebrated between two people in the presence and with the seal of God. The secret to the success of an alliance is brokenness. Only broken people will be able to relate at the alliance level. Brokenness is a spiritual attitude that can only happen with people who are crucified with Christ.

THE PRINCIPLE OF AUTHORITY

God is the origin of all authority. There are Classes of authority; natural, legal, and spiritual. When it is natural, you get coverage from your parents and even older siblings. When it is legal, you get it from government institutions like schools, teachers, from the city like the mayor or president. And when it is spiritual, you receive the covering of the shepherds. God established his spiritual coverage through the five ministries of Apostolic Authority. They are the Apostles, Prophets, Evangelists, Pastors, and Teachers for the edification of the Body of Christ. (See Ephesians 4:11), The Roman centurion was able to recognize the authority of Jesus the Christ because he himself had the experience of being under authority, which came from Rome while that of Jesus emanated from God himself.

From this scripture passage, we learn the double effect of authority; whoever is under authority exercises control over others. The Principle of authority is that "the greatest bless the least" (See Hebrews 7: 7): And without question, THE LESSER IS BLESSED BY THE GREATEST. (See Hebrews 6:13): For when God made the promise to Abraham, being unable to swear by another greater, he swore by himself, (Hebrews 6:16): *For men verily swear by the greater: and an oath for confirmation is to them an end of all strife.*

PRINCIPLE OF TRANSFER OF AUTHORITY

The power that a person has over another that is subordinate to him. God-given power to governor minister in the spiritual affairs of His People.

The kingdom of God is based on the principles of spiritual authority, and it is necessary to understand them so as not to fall under a curse. Since the one who motivates disobedience is Satan and not God, everyone who acts in disobedience is operating under

Satan's principles.

The transfer of authority is when God delegates power, the responsibility to a man who has all the support of God when exercising his ministry; likewise, when we obey such a person, we do not obey the man, but rather the authority placed on him.

EXAMPLES OF TRANSFER OF AUTHORITY

From Moses to Joshua ____ from Elijah to Elisha__ from the Father to Jesus Christ __from Jesus to his apostles. From Paul to Timothy.

In Matthew 8, we find the experience that Christ had with the Roman centurion. The centurion asked him to minister to his servant, who was ill. Christ told him that he would go to his house to heal him. But look what the centurion replied in (Matthew 8: 8-10)" *The centurion answered and said, Lord, I am not worthy to have you come under my roof; just say the word, and my servant will heal. For I too am a man under authority, and have under my command soldiers; And I say to this one: Go, and go; and to the other: Come and come; and to my servant: Do this, and it does. When Jesus heard this, he marveled and said to those who followed him, "Truly, I say to you, not even in Israel have I found so much faith."* The centurion recognized Christ as one under authority equal to him. He understood the Principle that authority does not come from our talent or calling.

OUR AUTHORITY COMES BECAUSE WE ARE UNDER AUTHORITY

It was the centurion's truth, and it was the truth with Christ Himself. The servant is not greater than his Lord is. Another who is already established in authority delegates the authority.

Christ did not deny what the centurion said. On the contrary, he affirmed what he said, and with a sent word, he healed the servant. It is one thing to have a call to a particular ministry. The call indicates what our potential is in Christ. But it is an entirely different matter to be prepared, recognized, authorized, delegated, and sent under authority. The call is the promise, but there are several steps before the fulfillment. The commissioning comes because the person has passed the tests and the preparation process. He is one who has been found faithful over a little so that he can then be put over much (See Matthew 25:21.)

THE NEED FOR PATERNITY IN COVERAGE

We are warmed by the relationship in the cold hours of the walk, it is better to be two than one because in the cold one warms the other. We know that leadership sometimes leads us to loneliness and isolation, there are many struggles, and we often prefer to internalize things because we understand that no one can help us, not even the most intimate person. In moments like this, we will experience the importance of having a spiritual father, someone truly spiritual and who can listen to our pains and nurture us to continue. (See1 Corinthians 4: 14-17.)

Generally, when we talk about spiritual fatherhood in the Body of Christ, we think exclusively of bringing someone to the Lord's way. Although this definition can be considered precise, in a certain way, it lacks its real meaning.

In the natural, when the man has participated in the gestation of a new being, and he is born from his mother's womb, technically, he is a "father." A father is also considered someone who not only puts the "seed" in the baby's conception but is also in charge of its subsequent education and maintenance.

If this is true in the natural sphere, how much more in the spiritual sphere? Just as biological children need a father to protect them, instruct them, provide for them, and bless them; spiritual children also need protection, provision, and coverage.

The concept of spiritual fatherhood is an ancient concept that predates Moses's time. Today we consider it part of God's plan for the integral formation of the Christian, including his training to serve the Lord in the local church's context.

In reality, our modern concept of leadership training fails significantly because we are not begetting future spiritual leaders (or servants?). When we send our potential future leaders to Bible institutes or seminars, we hope that the teachers there will prepare them for ministry.

We do this as part of a religious system without asking ourselves if we are doing the right thing. However, the Bible shows that Christianity is not a religion, but an intimate relationship with God the Father, through his Son Jesus Christ.

Therefore, if our faith is to focus on an intimate relationship with God, but we remove the "relationship" aspect in the process of ministerial training, we are straying from a biblical understanding of who our God is. To put it more clearly, we are ignoring to follow the example of our Lord Jesus Christ.

Coverage is not government

Spiritual coverage is paternity because whoever covers it will always seek to advise and guide, but to know that who should make the decisions is the one who is being covered. Having coverage is knowing that you have, above all, a real friend with whom you can confidently open your heart. Your coverage should tell you everything you think should be said without worrying whether it will please you or not, but it will do it in a respectful and loving way. Your coverage should not be afraid to tell you the truth, even if it means pointing out your mistakes, if necessary.

THE LEGITIMATE COVERAGE

This defines the real authority that comes from God through Jesus' Messianic Ministry by delegating authority to his Apostles and to the elders of the church. (See Ephesians 2:20): built on the foundation of the apostles and prophets, the main cornerstone being Jesus Christ himself, (Ephesians 4:11):"*And he himself constituted some, apostles; to others, prophets; to others, evangelists; to others, pastors and teachers.*" This legitimate coverage begins in Jerusalem as the seat of the church of Christ to the entire world, and after the apostles, it was transmitted to their disciples such as Timothy, Titus, Philemon, Luke, etc. But such an apostolic succession was interrupted by the persecutions and annihilation of the apostles and their disciples.

The church achieved this succession only in the first century, but after it was interrupted, apostasy infiltrated the church and since then reigned in confusion, ignoring the Nation of Israel as God's people, changing Jerusalem's seat to Rome, and introducing heretical doctrines.

The church lasted for several centuries until the second harvest of Pentecost arrived in the year 1900 in the great revival of Azusa, with the restoration of the Apostolic Church with its doctrines of Oneness and baptism of the Holy Spirit. However, it was necessary to restore the coverage of the legitimate authority of the church through apostles and prophets who in turn were recognized by The Jerusalem Church since the majority of churches (denominations) have arisen without such coverage, which prevented the complete restoration so that the church is complete and ready to receive the Lord at his second coming. (Psalms 122: 5): *"For there are set thrones of judgment, the thrones of the house of David."*

Coverage is not dictatorship

Spiritual coverage is not a dictatorship. Although we have news of coverage relationships that look more like a dictatorship, it is a distortion of the Principle and the real purpose of spiritual coverage. Although it is a relationship in which the covered person has spiritual authority over who is being covered, the exercise of that authority must always be done respecting the individuality and autonomy of the person who proposes to be covered.

WHAT IS THE CHURCH WITH LEGITIMATE AUTHORITY?

To answer this question, I will say that it is the church that recognizes Israel's people as the legitimate and original people of God and that is also willing to enter under his coverage. Do Christian denominations have no legitimate authority? To answer that first, I take you to the reflection of why there are so many denominations! The church of Christ is made up of Jews and Gentiles converted to Israel's God through the Messiah. Why is there so much confusion of creeds and denominations if we come from a single faith and from the same church? The answer is straightforward; apostolic succession was lost. No church can prove its legitimacy in succession; all denominations started with a foreign history to the original church.

CODE OF ETHICS IN COVERAGE

Spiritual coverage has a code of ethics, with some rules that both parties must respect in order for the results to be the best. I present the principles of effective coverage.

1) Those who enter coverage assume the commitment to be shepherded and mentored. Those who seek coverage accept being

shepherded and disciplined by those who cover them. The covered person puts himself in the humble position of someone who doesn't know everything and is open to learning.

2) Whoever enters coverage is willing to walk in transparency - To be transparent is to walk in the light. Transparency creates protection for the leader. Being transparent means having more personal and ministerial health.

3) Who covers should be free to minister in all areas of life and ministry of the person being covered - Whoever is protected should be open to receive ministry from the person who covers it so that they can oversee the various areas of their life and ministry.

4) Whoever is being covered agrees to be confronted - It is like spiritual coverage that there is a need for confrontation in some moments or situations. The confrontation is the great test that approves or disapproves of the independent one because he will hear things that, as a rule, no one would have the courage to say to him, and that may cause him pain. Rebuke hurts, but it brings healing.

UNDER COVERAGE

The Bible fundamentally teaches that we must be under spiritual coverage, children under the authority of their parents, citizens obeying their rulers, and fulfilling society's rules. The ministers of the Lord must also move under the delegated authority of God in a church. Authority from God must be covered. For example, a child who becomes an orphan without his parents' shelter and does not learn to obey, when forming his own family, will lack the values and principles to govern his house well and provide Adequate coverage for their children. That is one reason why many marriages fail because they come in turn from dysfunctional families or overprotective parents who have the trauma of family abuse or wealthy parents who give everything excessively to their children. After all, they were impoverished children before, etc. A pastor who is not subject to another senior pastor to live in obedience and accountability but is anarchic, independent, autonomous, with what authority will govern the church of Christ. How can you demand that the conscience of the faithful give their tithes if they do not give them to their pastor?

The Principle of Melchizedek

I already explained the Principle of authority that "the greatest blesses the least," but now I will teach you what I call "the principle of Melchizedek." This Principle is to tithe God in the right way; since many Pastors ignore this Principle and tithe in their churches, taking the money back to themselves or using it in the construction of their temple or giving it to the poor, none of these ways it's correct.

(Hebrews 7: 1): *For this Melchisedec, king of Salem, priest of the most high God, who met Abraham returning from the slaughter of the kings, and blessed him*; to whom Abraham also gave tithes of all; whose name means King of justice, and also King of Salem, that is, King of peace;(Hebrews 7: 4) *Consider how great this man was, to whom even the patriarch Abraham gave tithes of the spoil*. This passage clearly shows us the Principle of adequately decimating whom God has established as an authority.

Tithing to Melchizedek consists of the fruit of obedience to God's word in giving tithes to someone greater than oneself who gives us spiritual coverage, which consists of shepherding us, praying for the saints, supervising his congregation, giving accounts of his stewardship, and watching over their spiritual health.

If you are a Pastor and you are not covered, then where does your authority come from? If you don't know how to tithe but teach tithing to your congregation, don't you think it's dishonest?

It is not strange that many pastors stumble in situations and errors and that they suffer division in their churches because perhaps they divided themselves before and are reaping the fruit of their rebellion or their coverage is not a blessing! Maybe they opted for coverage that offered them financial support, and that is the only "non-legitimate" cause for which they are in that denomination; if so, they are not ministers of Christ but of men.

On the other hand, if you are a believer and are not spiritually covered, you do not have a pastor who covers you, go from church to church without belonging to any, are not committed, and not pleasing to God.

11

SPIRITUAL FATHERHOOD BREAKS BARRIERS

Every Father, every mother, dreams of begetting their children in the spirit. Children of his love and his blood. But children who also have engraved their very soul, their feelings, their yearnings. Children who possess their same depth, their same inner strength.

The prophetic word (**Rhema**) is the sword of the spirit according to (Ephesians 6:17). As such, it can bring great benefit, freedom, and edification. But in the hands of someone acting like a donkey without a rope, it can cause much damage.

God is maturing the prophetic and apostolic movement. We do not want a sword of the spirit, we need a religious formality that extinguishes God's fire, but we do need a form, an established protocol that can allow what is of God to flow and at the same time prevent those who only want to harm. One of the necessary things is spiritual coverage.

When Christ started His Church, He instituted the five ministries - not just one. These five ministries, when combined, represent the ministry of Christ to His Church. Each of these five ministries represents only a fifth of the anointing and ministry of Christ. Is neither complete nor independent of others, and all need to be under the direction of Christ to minister effectively. These five ministries must function as a team to edify the church and perfect it for the ministry's work.

Having spiritual coverage is more than just being a member of a congregation or having a certificate of ordination. I know of many who have a certificate of ordination, but their leaders don't know anything about them or what they do. I know many members of congregations who never submit to anyone.

Spiritual coverage implies that we have a relationship with our leaders. The lines of communication are open. It means that we are properly and healthily connected to the rest of the Body of Christ. It means that we honor others and allow them to give us feedback on our lives and even correction when necessary. Coverage implies that we are not a law to ourselves but accountable to others who are also under the Lordship of Christ

Jesus.

Spiritual covering is a protection to us and to those to whom we minister. I know that if at any time if I needed defense, I have Apostle Guillermo Maldonado and a whole network of King Jesus Ministries who would be by my side.

I also know that if I were in error, they would be by my side to correct and restore me. My coverage knows where I am and what I am doing because we have communication between us.

Most of the communication is the reports that I send myself and the tithes and offerings that I send to honor my authority. When preaching in other ministers, there are also the reports of the host pastors from whom I have ministered that are sent privately to my authority so that they know how it went from the perspective of the pastors who invited me. When I have questions or consider a change, I send them a message to see if they agree.

One of the benefits of spiritual fatherhood is that through it, spiritual children are introduced into God's ministry in a powerful way! Spiritual children receive by transfer everything that the father has received, that is, everything that the father received in revelation through sacrifices, trials, and struggles, the son gets simply by transfer! How great is God's grace! From this point, the son will begin his journey and move towards greater revelation in God by fulfilling the Word of God that says that His church will be transformed from glory to glory until it is ready for the wedding of the lamb! Perfect church, without wrinkles and spots, waiting for Jesus! We need to understand and work so that the generation that comes from us is better than ours. That is the Word that says: *"The memory of the righteous remains forever" (Psalm 112: 6), "The seed of the righteous will be powerful in the earth"* (Psalm 112: 2).

Another critical example where we can observe the principle of transference, where the father transfers "power" to the son, refers to the right to birthright among the Hebrew people. The birthright was highly valued among the Hebrews since the firstborn had some privileges after the death of his father, such as the right to exercise the priesthood in the family, the double portion of the paternal inheritance, authority over the younger brothers, title and power of the dad. We can see the importance of the birthright in Esau and Jacob's Biblical story, where the transfer of the birthright is done to Jacob.

Another benefit of being under coverage is that members participate in the anointing carried by that ministry. (See Psalms (133: 1-2). The anointing poured on the head flows and descends on every member of the ministry. This principle applies to all churches, be it the anointing that bears positive or negative. We reproduce (both spiritually and physically) according to our gender.

I know of a particular ministry that was very legalistic, closed, and contentious. When the founder passed away and did not name a successor, the churches' network suddenly fell apart because everyone wanted to be the next leader superior to the rest. The one network of churches was divided into four, but those four continued dividing into more. There are now close to twenty legalistic, closed, and contentious groups - each stealing sheep from the others, no one honoring anyone, all seeking their own, each proclaiming himself more significant than the others. The most astonishing result has been a shame on the Gospel. Of Jesus. The anointing that was on the prominent leader was reproduced in his children.

I want to encourage you, reader friend, find someone worthy of imitation, someone who imitates Christ - and follow him. Submit to the authority God has given you. Give honor to whom honor is due. Keep serving Christ willingly. When it is time for the door to open, God can open it - you will not have to force it.

A LEADER WHO HAS NO SPIRITUAL COVERAGE OVER HIM IS VERY DANGEROUS

For many years the church, consciously or unconsciously, put aside the Apostolic and prophetic ministries carrying a lack of authority spiritual in the world. Having cut two equipment ministries such as mentioned, left the Church "limping" and incomplete in important facets of its preparation for the dominion that God has destined her to exercise on earth. In synthesis, it is like conforming to a hand with five fingers, only working with three, pretending to consider it complete. Simultaneously, the church is a victim of a large sectorization due to contradictory theological positions and ideas.

This reality brought about a deterioration in their work and the impossibility of behaving as "one body," that of Christ. God has a plan, structure, and strategy for the body of Christ, the church, function, build, grow with a sense of destiny and fulfill the plan on earth through Apostles, prophets, evangelists, pastors, and teachers.

In (Ephesians 2:20) the word speaks to us that the foundation of apostles and prophets was the basis for the church to continue its development in the established order based on divine design.

We want to examine the leadership ministries that God has ordained in the body of Christ so that he may fulfill His purposes, hoping that we can see our need to submit to the Holy Spirit and the chain of authority that God has established in the church. By doing so, we are submitting to the Holy Spirit.

Everyone who has spiritual coverage receives the benefits of being protected, fed, and served as a source of blessing. Like sheep, many shepherds think that the leader is there to command as if was a foreman, but God chooses people to bless all His divine purposes and plans.

When we talk about Coverage, Apostles are pioneers. They have the character to reform, walk against religious currents, establish the church in the present truth, and return it to God's government.

The Genuine Apostles walk in the truth and not in the lie; they don't know they become Pharaohs who control the other ministries but take the parents' attitude and learn to release their spiritual children they conquest.

In these last times, God is powerfully restoring the ministry Apostolic, amid a fever of "apostolitis" where apostolic ministries have risen overnight that have hurt ministers and churches, especially with the theme of prosperity focused on support their ministries.

In these last days the body of Christ (the church) has ignored the importance and origin of the coverage; often, it is not ignorance in terms of knowledge, but better in terms of practicing this topic. A biblical principle is that from the beginning of all things, and before these, God was pleased to put, or constitute or place men to carry out His purposes, both heavenly and earthly.

What are the requirements to stay under spiritual coverage?

- Obedience to God and communion with Him and His word are required.
- Submission "be willing to give an account"
- Commitment and Loyalty to coverage
- It honors coverage (praying for it, giving respect, taking the vision of your coverage as your own, keeping with resources and words)
- Having covenant relationships

Lack of Fatherhood can create a chaos

Fatherhood alone is of paramount importance. The problem we face today in society with teenage pregnancy, drugs, lack of emotional instability, addictions, etc., is the remarkable absence of parents.

The absence of Spiritual Parents has caused significant problems for the Kingdom of God. This absence generates immature Christians, chained by vices and slaves to sin. They are like babies who are born but have no one to look after. The prophet Malachi speaks of this when he says: *"... to convert the hearts of parents to their children ... (Malachi 4: 6)"*. Today there is a clamor echoing for Spiritual Parents.

A family without a father is like that Tower of Pisa in Italy, a building that, although it took much effort to build, can never be perfect without an extraordinary divine action. Parents are spiritual and human references in their families and make all the difference; the absence of a father is like a puzzle without the main pieces. He is responsible for introducing the 'Lord to his family, bringing forth new fruits for the church.

The great antidote to the world's problems is holiness; each family's goal should be to climb the steps of Christian perfection together. The more families that aspire to this goal, the fewer tragedies happen, even natural disasters.

God's intention is to raise Spiritual Parents to help these children grow so that they impact families, the church, and society. This restoration of harmony between parents and children, both natural and spiritual, will allow the inheritance to be passed on to the next generations.

How to become a true, mature son, ready to receive the inheritance?

Elisha has a passion for God and sees his spiritual father as the means God uses to bless him (See Psalms 133: 1-3). It is clear that the man or woman of God who has been appointed to take care of them is the channel through which God will transmit all the spiritual inheritance (gifts, revelation, authority, anointing, etc.) that he will need to be efficient and effective in the call that God has made to you, and that will open the doors of fulfillment (joy) and prosperity in that call.

You have a real longing for your inheritance (See 2 Kings 2: 1-11, especially 2: 9). It is not like Esau who sells his inheritance for a plate of lentils (better opportunities, better titles, higher recognition, better income, greater comfort, Etc.), but like Jacob, who struggles hard to receive that inheritance. He does not allow any obstacle, including the spiritual father, to keep him from receiving that inheritance, like Elisha when Elijah tells him on three different occasions to leave him because God has sent him to other places.

He always has a great desire to be close to his spiritual father (See 2 Kings 2: 1-11). He always takes the initiative to seek a relationship with his spiritual father. He is not one of the people who are complaining all the time in the churches that the pastor ignores them, does not visit them, does not look for them, or does not speak to them. They create opportunities to be with the pastor.

He does not try to take his inheritance ahead of time but waits until his spiritual father gives it to him (Joshua, David, and Elisha). He does not try to take what is rightfully his by the wrong means, such as the arrogance of feeling more than his spiritual father, or division or rebellion. Neither pride nor rebellion nor division is a way to achieve God's blessing. Instead, they are cursing paths to become ineffective, ineffective, sterile, for the Lord (See Proverbs 16:25). Instead, learn to wait on the Lord in faith to receive your inheritance at the right time.

12

COVERING REVEALS PURPOSE

The authority that God has released for your church is making your purpose unfold. The spiritual authority must function as a priest (representative of God), as ahead of the organization (one who determines the goals/targets); as a father (we are the great family of God), the commitment of spiritual fatherhood is to our future. This authority releases into our lives protection, provision, prosperity, and perfection (improvement).

When you have a purpose, you know that you need to be in excellent health and a lot of energy to strive for your goal. However, when the purpose is lacking, there is also a reason to take care. You stop doing physical activities and taking care of the food. Soon comes overweight, excessive sleep, the desire to spend the day on the couch.

Your relationships are sidelined with a purpose

Having a purpose makes you feel good, and when you feel good; your relationships - with family, with your partner, with friends - flourish. On the other hand, if you do not have a purpose, you are unhappy, and your relationships reflect that.

You never have patience; you are not interested in listening to others because you are absorbed in your own unhappiness; spend time complaining and making negative comments. Nobody wants to be around someone like that! As a result, it does not take long for you to distance yourself from the people who matter to you.

One of the causes of the crisis facing the modern world and the church is the almost total absence of spiritual fatherhood that plagues us. We need spiritual fatherhood! If men who are supposed to practice spiritual fatherhood are spending their time practicing "spiritual contraception," so to speak, they cannot and will not be spiritually fruitful.

Some might say that spiritual coverage aims to show the person the way, protecting them from the ills of wrong decisions. However, the Bible is clear when it shows us that what shows us the way is the Word of God, because it is in it that all the will of God is found for us, and it is our rule of faith and practice: *"Indeed your testimonies are my pleasure, they are my counselors"* (Psalms119: 24). A person can make the decisions of his life only and exclusively by consulting the Word of God, without any need for third party approval.

Evidently, leaders and other brothers in Christ have a positive role in our lives, as each part of the body of Christ is important and contributes to the growth of the body (See Ephesians 4:16). We participate in each other's lives by counseling, helping, supporting, crying together, rejoicing together, etc. This is the existing human partnership based on love. (See Romans 8:26).

Your belief in God has given you security, salvation. Here you teach us that the advancement of our life depends on the spiritual authority that God has placed on your life. Every man must be subject to authority, and it will be the voice of God for his life.

"Truly, truly, I say to you, Whoever honors whoever I send, honors me; and whoever honors me, honors the one who sent me." (See John 13: 20). We are not changing the world but enhancing what God wanted to say.

Spiritual parents sent from God for our lives, and if we honor them as sent by the Lord, we will receive the reward of the function/anointing that works on that person.

The leader of that church has an honor for the authority that is over him. When you have a spiritual father, you have coverage. The spiritual Aba (father) is a position of someone who functions as a father. Some teach us, but others are our mentors. Abba is present in an observable way that we can imitate. Father in the Bible is not just a person who made us, but someone who will establish our purpose. It is a relationship of trust, which he considers his words. When God connects us with someone, it is because he wants to release something for us.

Being united is not just being together; each has its role. A part of the unit is each doing their part. The anointing comes from Christ. He is the head of the church. The beard is an expression of honor in the ministry. The anointing comes through the mechanism of the spiritual father. The spiritual father does not generate comfort in us but in preparation. *"Honor your father and your mother (which is the first commandment with a promise) so that it may be well with you and that you may have a long life on earth. And you, parents, do not provoke your children to wrath, but raise them in the discipline and admonition of the Lord."* (Ephesians 6: 2-4). This honor also involves the spiritual fatherhood that God has placed on your life.

ADVANTAGES OF SPIRITUAL COVERAGE

When we connect with a spiritual father:
- Knowledge arrives
- The vision is broadened
- We gain identity
- Our individual purpose is released
- We receive the spiritual inheritance
- The anointing and supernatural resources are operating on your life.

Many problems that people face in the relationship stem

from the lack of coverage. Moreover, as they become adults and arrive at marriage, they are constantly plagued by fear. Women who imagine they are being betrayed by their spouse. Husbands who are extremely jealous. Teachers who do not love their disciples. Disciples are tired of their leaders.

Research shows that people have felt increasingly lonely. Did you know that 80% of people, who do plastic surgery, in less than two years, return to do another plastic surgery? It is as if dissatisfactions are eternal. People who do not feel covered and are looking for protection and self-acceptance.

As children of God, we have a call from the father: to make a difference in such a difficult world. We know the importance of coverage, and we need to teach the lost that it is still worthwhile to follow the principles of the Word, to teach them the importance of the coverage.

When a man has a sexual relationship with a woman, and she gives birth, technically, he is a father. All paternity comes from the father. But if you don't take care of that child, you are worse than an unbeliever. The Bible agrees with this concept: *"But if anyone does not provide for his own, and especially for those in his home, he has denied the faith and is worse than an unbeliever."* (1 Timothy 5: 8). Spiritual father in the body of Christ speaks of bringing someone to the Lord, or "born" to them in the Kingdom of God. Just as natural children, need a father to protect them, instruct them, provide for them, and bless them; spiritual children also need protection, provision, and blessings. The concept of fatherhood is very old and is part of God's plan for evangelism and ministerial training.

Every minister or family, to fulfill God's law of multiplying and being fruitful, must first give birth to children through the Gospel. To win souls is to beget children for the kingdom of God.

Paternity is manifested when we are providers to the children. A newborn child is someone so delicate and fragile that he requires our full attention and care; it needs spiritual milk to grow. (1Peter 2:2)"*Desire, like newborn children, the unadulterated spiritual milk, so that by it you may grow for salvation*," Every child requires a mother-father to provide him with food… Statistics say that many children die every day from malnutrition. The same thing happens in the spiritual field.

The author of spiritual coverage

Fatherhood is fellowship and reciprocal communion with his disciples. A minister takes one or more to train him and enable him for the ministry that the Lord has called him to do. Moses had a Joshua. Elijah had an Elisha. Paul had his Timothy. Jesus had his disciples. It is important to "walk together" for several reasons the spiritual father can watch over the life, character, and spiritual gifts of his spiritual son. The father can help correct and discipline his son, developing good character and the Fruits of the Spirit within him. The father can help recognize the special call of God, direct and prepare him for that specific work.

Fatherhood is anointing his (sons) disciples to send them to minister alone without Him. (John 20:21) "*Then Jesus said to them again: Peace be with you. As the father sent me, so I also send you.* "· A son recognizes the ministry of his –spiritual father -, he is not rebellious; he always goes out with his blessing to fulfill his duty. They stay connected to their spiritual parents. The child understands that he needs the continued prayers of his father to stay strong, focused, and protected. They do not act on their own. (Isaiah 30: 1) *Woe to the rebellious children, saith the LORD, that take counsel, but not of me; and that cover with a covering, but not of my spirit, that they may add sin to sin.*

Parents let us understand our responsibility for our spiritual children. Children recognize the importance of parenthood. Discipleship needs to be redefined as a commitment to "spiritual parenting," "spiritual nurturing," or "spiritual mentoring."

The willingness to be obediently positioned on leadership, spiritual parenting guides us in the ways of the Lord. The coverage of our leaders is one of the most important factors in developing God's purpose for us. For it is in unity that God works the blessing.

Our associations are so important in our journey because they are the people, we associate with that God uses to prepare us for what He has for us. Before we discover our purpose, we must discover the connections that lead us to them; even with call and anointing, we need mentors who prepare us for the fullness of this purpose of God. When we receive whom Jesus sent, it is as if we receive Jesus Himself. Then I will go down and speak to you there; I will take away the spirit that is upon you and put it on them; and they will carry the burden of the people with you, lest you take it alone.

The spiritual father is not the one who generated us biologically, but he is a source of inspiration and support. He is someone we can imitate, who acts as the mouth of God for our lives and prevents us from being disconnected from the source that is Jesus. His role is to exhort, correct, and transfer the anointing that works on your life to your disciples, activating your gifts. We must always honor the spiritual father whom God has appointed us because honor is what keeps the flow of anointing alive on us.

13

FATHERHOOD AND RESPONSIBILITY

Satan, in his careful plan to destroy the family, seeks to disparage the father's role. The increase in violence, youth crimes, great poverty and economic insecurity, the poor performance of an increasing number of children in our schools are clear evidence of the lack of positive influence from the father in the home. The family needs the father to anchor it.

The first commandment given to Adam and Eve by God referred to the potential to become parents, as husband and wife. We declare that the command given by God to His children, to multiply and fill the earth, remains in force. We also declare that God has ordained that the sacred powers of procreation should be employed only between man and woman, legally married.

We warn that people who violate chastity covenants, who mistreat their spouses or children, or who fail to fulfill their family responsibilities, must one day respond to God for fulfilling those obligations. We also warn that the disintegration of the family will cause the calamities predicted by ancient and modern prophets to fall on people, communities, and nations.

The lack of paternity causes many to submit to an abusive relationship. Others are averse to the subject of fatherhood in both the spiritual and the natural because of the abuse of authority. For this absence, many people are averse to the male reference. And in this cycle, chaos is installed due to lack of order. A fatherless family suffers spiritually both financially, socially, and psychologically.

There are many ways to be a father. There are those who have children with their own wife, and there are those who adopt children. It is very special to be a natural father. Embrace the children and have them close by, knowing that when we return home, they will be there waiting for us. But the fact is that by God's sovereignty, many are not natural parents and never will be. Nevertheless, all believers in Christ can indeed be spiritual parents, "parents in the faith" of sons and daughters. And just as there is a joy in the father's heart for having a child, there is also a lot of joy when we become spiritual fathers (or mothers) who brought people to the knowledge of Christ.

We know that the miracle of the new birth is only possible if God performs it, but we have a responsibility to direct people's steps towards God, the Eternal Father; although there are, unfortunately, no guarantees that our children will stick to what they have been taught. It is important to remember that children are not objects without their own will. Rather, they are human beings who, as adults, will make their own choices. Nevertheless, the risk is less when they are well oriented and are established since childhood in the Word of God. Hence the importance of the believing father in running his home. Thus, this great challenge remains for all of us. We may never have the opportunity to generate natural children, but we will always have the possibility to generate spiritual children who live for the glory of God. And if we are parents of natural children, we have this dual responsibility, both to guide our own and to announce the kingdom, thus increasing the heavenly nursery.

To talk about parenting is to talk about family, and to talk about family is to talk about diversity. Each person had or has a type of relationship with the father that is demonstrated by the positioning towards the relationships. There are people who have always had a father, caregiver, defender, provider, loving, counselor, friend, etc. Others, quite the reverse, a father who forsaken, did not provide education, food, the son grew up without parental advice and was discredited, that is, he does not have an ideal father reference and many times these relationships reflect in our way of relating to God and with the people.

Carnal parents have a responsibility to care for, teach values and how to deal with certain situations, provide food, basic care for their child's development, and spiritually we also need to live this.

On your spiritual journey, who is your father now? Who cares and believes in you?

We all have people who help us in the first steps on the Christian walk, just as we also have people who help us in the first steps in our biological growth until we can walk with our own legs, but even as we grow and mature, we will have a human reference in our lives, and for many, this is the father, but for many, the truth is that they suffer from orphanhood and may die, suffer a lot due to lack of direction from a spiritual father or even fail to achieve benefits from advice from a person who has already experienced difficulties that could be avoided.

The spiritual paternity relationship is for people who have the courage to open to more intense discipleship, not just based on meetings, cells, teaching, barbecues, outings, etc. Although it is very important and indispensable, paternity gives the right and duties of spiritual parents and children who have assumed this type of relationship.

On the other hand, the spiritual father also has his duties as a father. It is a relationship of reciprocity, I take care and am taken care of, sowing respect and being respected and passing the values from father to son by example, that is, family relationship between brothers in Christ and spiritual parents reflect the Person of God, this is family, this is God's project. You must count on your spiritual father to cry together, to rejoice together, to see the father organizing the Christian family promoting love, unity, growth among the brothers, etc.

"I do not write these things to shame you, but I admonish you as my beloved children. For though you had ten thousand teachers in Christ, you would not, however, have many parents; because, by the gospel, I have begotten you in Jesus Christ. Therefore, I admonish you to be my imitators." (I Corinthians 4: 14-16)

We are beloved children of God, and as leaders, while we are children; we are spiritual parents of spiritual children. Therefore, our concern for the children that the father has given us is to take care of them in all areas. As a disciple, do you know where your disciple lives? When was the last time you visited? Do you know if he is in need?

These questions are of discipleship; the spiritual father adds the function of knowing with whom he relates, his friendships, what must be done to help him, to demand positioning, where he walks, and what and how he speaks. It is the role of the leader, as a father, to know where his children are going.

When Paul sent his spiritual children, they were his representatives; it was Paul in them. The most important title for God is that of a son because no matter what the person is when he becomes a son of God, everything can be changed (See John 1.12). Many leaders cannot generate children because they did not have parents, but God wants to heal their spiritual sterility. We can see that Jesus taught us that the Father seeks true worshipers, being thus before any definition, the worshiper must be a child of God.

No matter what happened in your life regarding human parenting, don't compare who God is with who people are, and everyone who wants to be a good spiritual father is inspired by the One and Eternal Father of us all: God the Creator. After all, we don't replace Him; we reflect Him. May we reflect this paternity of love and build lives as a good father builds the lives of his children, forming a healthy family, with healthy brothers and relationships that reflect the presence of God, with people healed, loved, and healed in their existential diseases.

All responsible parents wish the best for their children. But the complexity of human relationships sometimes makes it difficult, in some situations, to determine what, in fact, the best we really want means.

Being a father depends on being a mother for the exercise of paternity, with the responsibility of two hearts that interact with loving the creature generated by both. The father and the mother's mutual and generational love makes the children learn that love in-depth is plural and complementary in the conjugation of man and woman. So, membership has a full passion for masculinity and femininity. Adoption membership also finds this ideal echo of love in the learning of father and mother.

Jesus, the Son of God, has always shown his intimate loving relationship with the father, especially with his moments of special prayers with Him in places apart from the people. He also wanted to show, in a human way, his connection with his mother and adoptive father, who always acted in accordance with the will of the Father God. Before her marriage to Joseph, Mary manifested herself to the angel with the desire to fulfill what God wanted from her. He accepted the marriage to give the child that would have the warmth of the ideal home for his son.

The wisdom of God is madness for man because those who do not know Him cannot call Him a Father and consequently do not understand what it is to be a child of God. As we participate in the Kingdom of God, through Jesus, we are able to live with God and then have homes. God would not give us the conditions to be children if the condition did not exist and we lived with our father. God is organized and has always prepared the address for all his children so that everyone can live with Him.

In my father's house, there are many mansions; if it were not so, I would have told you. I will prepare a place for you. (John 14:2). Imagine the joy of a son who, after years, had the opportunity to meet his father. This joy is the representation of what we feel when we start a relationship between Father and Son with God. But to know him, it is not enough to call him a FATHER. To know God, we need to relate to Him. And how do we do that? With the reading of the Word of God and prayer. Only through this, can we recognize and know God. His word is the truth, and it alone sets us free.

Holiness is a consequence of when we relate to God. As we

establish that contact, we increasingly need to be clean and pure to worship God. In addition, sanctification is a Christian's responsibility. We must seek it constantly. *Having therefore these promises, dearly beloved, let us cleanse ourselves from all filthiness of the flesh and spirit, perfecting holiness in the fear of God.* (2 Corinthians 7: 1.)

IMPORTANCE OF AUTHORITY

In order to understand the importance of authority, it is necessary to understand that God puts authority with a purpose and that when one does not accept authority, then it brings condemnation because it resists the established or desired by God. The principle that the Apostle Paul manages in this passage is with the delegated authorities, not with the direct authority of God. This indicates, if I don't accept the authority I see, it's a lie that I'm under authority, which I don't see. Therefore, if I want to submit to the authority I see, it is necessary to have a meeting first, with the authority I do not see. Therefore, if I do not submit to the delegated authorities, it is a symptom that I am not in communion with God.

Many people and relationships are affected by a lack of recognizing authority. In the world, equality is being preached, and the freedom of the people, this is fine as long as equality does not encompass authority, and the freedom that the world demands does not violate the moral, spiritual, and regulations of marriage, home, etc. Rather, I think there should be some educational system, which teaches society, everyone who takes their rightful place, in church, family, at work, school, or elsewhere because it sounds like people speak evil of their leaders, employers, teachers, husbands, parents, and even pastors. If there were more humility and obedience in the world than is needed, for our environment to be better conducted, everything would be different. There would be more health, cleanliness, prosperity, love, and unity.

The kingdom of God is based on his authority.

One of the main things we must know is that the kingdom of God is Spiritual, and therefore settles in our hearts before settling on earth. Let us see what it says in the bible. In (John 18:36) Jesus answered: *My kingdom is not of this world; if my kingdom were of this world, my servants would fight so that I would not be handed over to the Jews; but my kingdom is not from here*. This makes it clear that only those who walk in the spirit can function, within the kingdom of God, for the bible says: (John 3:5) Jesus answered: *True, I say unto you, that he that is not born of water and the spirit cannot enter the kingdom of God*. Thus, the function within the kingdom of God is by revelation, not by human understanding. Therefore, Jesus told his disciples to ask that the kingdom be established in their lives. (Luke 11:2) In addition, he said unto them, *When ye pray, say, Our Father which art in heaven, Hallowed be thy name. Thy kingdom come. Thy will be done, as in heaven, so in earth*. So, before we can establish the kingdom of God on earth, it has to be established in our hearts, to respond with obedience, as long as he calls us.

Authority is a central theme in all areas of life. We honor authority out of respect for God, for his authority, and for his purposes. We seek to be free from all forms of disrespect to the authorities, out of love and reverence for our father. Submission and authority are spiritual realities (See Ephesians. 5:20-21). A spiritual person can see God's hand on weak people who possess delegated authority.

THE GOD OF ORDER

One of the things we should know is that God is order, so if he established his church, then he did it in order. (See Ephesians 4:11-12). God establishes the ministries mentioned here for the church's proper functioning, within an order. But here we see, that obedience to these ministers is necessary, so that the kingdom of God may be established on earth, for one of the functions of these ministries is to prepare, or to empower the saints to serve God, but without obedience, this work cannot be possible. Therefore, the body of Christ is not built, for lack of obedience to the authorities delegated by God. The problem goes further, for the bible says. (Romans 13:2) *"So whoever opposes authority, to the established by God resists; and those who resist, bring condemnation to themselves"*. Here we can see that this is resistance to God's will and that, as a result, it entails condemnation to those who resist, not only cannot the body of Christ be built, but also this one is unable to serve God.

Dishonoring authority is one of Satan's main actions.

Sacrifice without obedience to authority seeks to serve God in the same spirit as the spirit by which Satan rules his kingdom. Cain, Saul, Nadab, Abihu offered sacrifices to God while neglecting God's authority (See Genesis 4:1-8). Their sacrifices were rejected. Obedience to God, His Word, and His authority are more important to God than our sacrifices in ministry. Without understanding this, many seek to serve God by making sacrifices, without ever solving in their lives the realm of honor of obedience to His authority (at home, at work, in the church, or in the nation).

THE BACKGROUND OF REBELLION

For us to understand, because it is that the church, or the saints, are unable to accuse of disobedience, it is necessary to understand where rebellion is born (See Isaiah 14:12-14). In Satan, Rebellion is born, for it was he who revealed himself against the authority of God, and that seed is the one that sows in man, that it may be revealed against all that God wants. When operating on a principle of disobedience, it is working on the wrong side, and the devil knows this, so it inhibits our lives against God's will to gain right over us. This is why the bible says that we bring condemnation to us. Here is another question, how does this happen?

The devil uses the same method that brought him down. (See Ezekiel 28:12*)*. This passage explains who Satan was before, and describes him as a perfect being, full of wisdom, finished in beauty and inhabited the mount of God, but what happened? This passage also recounts that because of his beauty, his heart was eternal, and because of his splendor corrupted his wisdom. When Satan looked at himself, he thought that he was equal to God, but he was forgotten, that he was only a created being. This happened because he was intoxicated with arrogance, and as a result, it was revealed against who he believed was equal to him, or perhaps I came to think that he was inferior to him. Here I would like to mention that this is the basis of the rebellion to believe that we are superior to the leader. We may be, but the calling rests not upon us but on the leader. We cannot comprehend that we are under his authority, by God's will, for his work to grow. On the other hand, Satan, full of thoughts of pride in our hearts, telling us that we are better and that we do not have to be under his authority.

Disobedience to delegated authority - disobedience to God's will

Let us remember that the bible says that whoever opposes authority to God's established resists is because his kingdom works in authority while the kingdom of darkness works in rebellion. (See Matthew 21:33-41).

This passage clearly illustrates how delegated authority works, for the Lord sent his servants on behalf of him, but the husbandmen did not respect them, for one of the owner's son was killed. Nevertheless, when the work owner comes, which is the church, and then judgment will come upon them for not respecting their representatives. They did not appreciate them, because with that acrimony they won, because no one told them anything. Many today in church, do not hold the proper authority because they want to do what they want.

ORDER IN THE KINGDOM

When God established authorities in the church, He did so to operate through them. (See Hebrews 13:17). Let us see what the bible says in (Revelation 2:1) *"Write to the angel of the church in Ephesus: He who has the seven stars in his right hand, who walks amid the seven golden candlesticks"* In this passage, the word angel, comes from the Greek angel messenger, angel, sent. This phrase is repeated in the churches, and by definition of the word, it is believed that it refers to the pastor of the churches.

On the other hand, it can be said that the pastor is the earthly head of the church, to which God addresses, for he is responsible. But what happens when God brings a vision about a place, and people do not obey but rebel against the leader because they do not want to be uncomfortable? For the kingdom is affected, and God's will cannot be established. Here is the importance of obedience.

Honor Spiritual authority is a requirement

God commands us not to gossip against our leaders, at home, in the church, in society (See Exodus. 22:28; Acts. 23:5).

God commands us this because he honors his authority, the one he has delegated to those responsible: the unity of families, at work, in the church, and society. To sin against a leader is to sin against unity. To sin against unity is to sin against God's designs for the group concerned. Jesus answered the priest who was not converted out of respect for authority (See Matthew. 26:62-64). Jesus encouraged Cesar to pay taxes; it was a declaration of submission to authority.

Paul respects the same priest who helped organize the crucifixion of Jesus. Paul repents for having had strong words because he represented the authority of God: And Paul said:" *I did not know, brethren, that he was the high priest: for it is written: You shall not speak ill of the leader of your people."*(Acts. 23:5).

When we feel mistreated, we should first talk to God, then to the one who mistreated us, and then to those responsible who have the authority to bring a solution. Sharing an offense to a friend who is not in a position to carry a solution is slander. God commands leaders to remove those who slander from the community after allowing them to repent. God gives this commandment because those who slander sin against the unity of the body. The church has the right to receive a charge against a leader, only if it is based on two or three witnesses. (See 1 Timothy. 5:19.)

THE SOURCE OF AUTHORITY

Clearly, as pastors, leaders, and intercessors, we all need to work with greater authority. Yet even though we enjoy a variety of graces that build us personally, God gives us authority for a specific purpose: to accomplish His purposes on earth. What are they? One of these heavenly purposes is found in the sending of the disciples made by Jesus. "*All authority has been given to me in heaven as on earth. Go and make all nations disciples."* (Matthew. 28. 18, 19).

Christ gave the church the authority to make disciples. We have been much more successful in making converts than disciples. Today, many believe in Jesus, but few are indeed followers of Christ. We must take our converts and teach them "*to keep all the commandments of Jesus*" (v. 20). When the church returns to teaching Jesus and teaches it, our disciples will have the authority to do everything Jesus did.

However, spiritual authority is not something we possess simply because we struggle to have it. We cannot buy it as Simon had tried to do (See Acts 8. 18). The power of authority does not work simply because we copy another's methods, such as the sons of Scéva (See Acts 19:14-16). Nor can it be automatically obtained because we read books on how to build the church. When we focus on obedience to Christ's words, His authority is revealed in our lives.

Since the day of our salvation, we have been the object of the Unconditional Love of the Father. However, as we mature, we realize that there comes a time when the father's love for us seems conditional. It was the case for Christ, as is the case with those who follow Him. He said, "*For this reason the Father loves me, because I give my life.*" (John 10. 17.)

Jesus lived in the most profound intimacy of the father's love because He gave His life for the sheep. If we want to grow in real authority, we must give our lives for His sheep.

As leaders, we need an administrative authority because of our position within the church. However, spiritual authority transcends administrative authority. It is the path of proper spiritual authority: in full possession of our souls, without fear of being intimidated by an external source, we choose to give our lives for the sheep of Christ. Completely free, with many and visible possibilities to escape this commitment, we offer our souls without fear to God. No one controls us but God, yet our lives are offered, like Christ's, in intercession for others. When we are subjected to unjust opposition, we endure silently, and it is in these moments that spiritual authority enters our lives.

14

THE FATHERHOOD WITH GUILLERMO MALDONADO

Nowadays church is not reaching many of the lost, sick, and hurting because believers become too religious and cannot take the authority and power they have been given through Christ. After years of being in church but never understood my identity in the spirit realm, I made a step of faith through my spiritual father, Apostle Guillermo Maldonado of King Jesus Ministry, to confirm the real message found in (Malachi 4: 6) with a specific focus on the relationships between fathers- children. Of all the things that Malachi could have told us about the preaching of the future "Elijah," he chooses to tell us "*He will turn the hearts of fathers to their children and the hearts of children to their fathers, lest I come and smite the land with a curse*".

I was raised in church and did all things as regular Christian would do but never experienced the power of God and demonstrated what Jesus said in His word: "*And these signs will accompany those who believe: In my name, they will drive out demons; they will speak in new tongues; they will pick up snakes with their hands; and when they drink deadly poison, it will not hurt them at all; they will place their hands on sick people, and they will get well.*" (Mark 16:17-18).

I have decided to join the movement of the glory of God, which is transforming me. I have refused to live a religious mindset but instead to collaborate with Apostle Maldonado and his vision to expand the kingdom of God, bring the supernatural power to this generation, and raise sons and daughters across the globe.

Through Apostle Maldonado's persistent message on the supernatural and his hunger for souls, I was able to understand now it was time for religion to stop substituting for God's power. God's supernatural presence is to protect you from the devil's deception; learn to hear God's voice; overcome demonic attacks; understand how to operate in the supernatural. I become the carrier of God's power, and I have the flow of energy and as Jesus wherever I walk, I carry His power, and in His name, miracles, wonders, and signs are possible.

My respect for him is immeasurable. With a sharp mind and a tender heart, the Apostle has faithfully served his church for more than 20 years. Without his vision for church planting, his willingness to invest in me as a pastor, and his steady commitment to our church, we would not exist.

A charismatic spiritual father

I have found in Apostle Guillermo Maldonado, a charismatic spiritual father. I did not know the meaning of a spiritual father when I first joined King Jesus Ministry. I did not have a good relationship with my biological father. He was more about punishment for any error made. When the first time I met Apostle Maldonado, and he called me son, I felt different. I found a genuine spiritual father in him, and his care was more relational and not something systematized.

Like Jesus, I have been observed the Apostle as a real spiritual father to his disciples, who cared for them, taught them, and disciplined them. At the same time, he did not control them, so that even other disciples he helped. They were free to leave without cursing them. He never controlled them, but he did care, and he did speak the truth. The true spiritual father cares and watches over people as though they are the real children. Because of his love and integrity, he pushed the disciples to excellence. There is a genuine relational connection with him where you find a sense of belonging and care between each other.

The Apostle Guillermo Maldonado's relationship with his spiritual children is genuine as Elijah was a spiritual father to Elisha – it was an honest relationship. Moses was a spiritual father to Joshua, another real relationship.

True spiritual fathers want what is best for those they care for and will sacrifice and pray for those under their care. However, real spiritual children have the same corresponding attitude toward the father, they care and are not taking advantage of him.

During my tenure as pastor under Apostle Guillermo Maldonado's covering, I found he has been a caring spiritual father, a charismatic spiritual father, or an influential or powerful spiritual father. I observed him, and I have applied his teaching in my daily life wherein a short period after he sent me out, I have been able to secure our church property with a growing ministry in a problematic area where most ministers failed.

Obedience to a spiritual father kept the disciples under the Apostle King Jesus Ministry's covering away from pride and independence, keeping their steps oriented towards the Lord. Because of my obedience to the Apostle Maldonado, I desire to reproduce the same attitude in my spiritual children and transmit what I have received from my spiritual father, who urged us to go beyond what he taught us. Parents want their children to be an extension of their ministry and have even more than they have. One way to multiply is to have many children who reproduce their anointing and call.

Suppose something important in the spiritual father I have caught from the Apostle has been his prayer life. Another fundamental key of every true spiritual father is his life of prayer for the children entrusted to him. A sign of the great love that moved the ministry is, without doubt, his intercessory prayer.

He has been a massive encouragement, regularly challenging me to leave fear and shame behind and to embrace the power of God's Spirit to move toward love, self-control, and a willingness to share in Christ's sufferings.

The love of Spiritual Father

Right now, there are people in your life who are desperate for a father figure. They are looking for godly men who are of godly examples. I had pastored for almost seven years before the idea of spiritual fatherhood towards others became a reality in my life. I was preparing the message of "Father's Day" five years ago when The LORD revealed to me that there were people in my congregation looking for me as a "spiritual" father. I had become a "dad" in faith for them. They saw me as a father as much as my biological children did.

I don't share these comments to flatter myself. God forbids! I share them to help all men realize that people seek us as the example of our heavenly father. It still amazes me that people see me that way. I am also learning to participate in that role through faith and be the father I am called to be.

Never underestimate the power of parenthood. Never minimize the parents' need. Our children are crying out for them; Adults live their lives starving for love, approval, and acceptance from the father. The need for true parents is real, and it is impressive.

I have traveled the world preaching, and Wherever I went, I always asked pastors the same question: "What is the greatest need you have in this country?" Most of them answered. "We need spiritual parents!"

END TIMES SPIRITUAL FATHER

Unfortunately, many men never realized how important this powerful call to spiritual fatherhood is. The Apostle Paul put it best in 1 Corinthians 4: 14-16 (NIV): "*I do not write these things to you to embarrass you, but to warn you. Even though they had ten thousand teachers to teach them about Christ, they only have one spiritual father. Well, I became their father in Christ Jesus when I preached the Good News to them. So I beg you to follow me.*"

I met a young man of 19 years old son of a single mother. His dad never recognized him nor cared for him. Until the age of eight, he was at his grandmother, after which his grandparents could no longer take care of him. With all the pain in his soul, his mother finally had to hand him over to a home for orphaned children. He escaped several times because he could not bear the strict regime and the lack of freedom, but the police took him back home. I met him at the church, and he agreed to become a disciple. He could have ended very badly, but because of the love as father I gave him, he became one of the faithful disciples; now, he is pursuing his college degrees.

Some of us will have had the grace to experience a good earthly father, others not. However, we are all called to transcend our personal history, mature a filial relationship with the Blessed Mother and Father God, and give the world our spiritual fatherhood and motherhood, a reflection of what is most characteristic of God. In this way, many other people will overcome their emotional wounds and anchor themselves deeply in a God who is above all-merciful father. Living that spiritual fatherhood is not easy. It requires much dedication.

CONCLUSION

Based on the previous chapters, we define "spiritual fatherhood" as the supernatural ability that God's children have to love their neighbor (even their enemies) as the father loves them, thus showing the love and image of God to others as Jesus did. A way of loving that distinguishes us from other human beings who have not known the Lord is what makes us his disciples. This love of the father or spiritual fatherhood that we must give to others is for believers a moral commandment that we must fulfill.

Being in Christ, this spiritual paternity can be exercised where Christians mature to reach the Lord's image. This love is not only the goal of Christian discipleship, but it is also the engine of discipleship, which leads us to reach the lost to make disciples and that in turn, they go out to do the same.

Everything you have received from his hand, everything you are and possess has been a gift from heaven; don't forget that without your father's blessing, you could end up in ruin in an instant; in this house, God gives you coverage, but you have to diligently and earnestly seek His blessings. The Lord supports the authorities He establishes and if your spiritual father stopped blessing you, believe me, you would soon be in trouble.

Spiritual fatherhood is part of our identity. It runs like DNA through our veins. It defines us as believers; it identifies us as heirs of the kingdom; we can have many children, but we have only spiritual parents; let them guide us and direct us because when we leave their cover, we also do it from the divine.

Many children are growing up without a father or mother or with a divided family, a drama that hinders access to the experience of a merciful God the Father. Regarding the fields of pastoral care and Christian life, we would propose to encourage grooming a vision of the meaning of fatherhood and motherhood in all its dimensions, both human and spiritual, fundamental mission of man and woman to help the Father to generate biological life, but also spiritual and wisdom. The accent we think should be on fatherhood since we consider it the most currently damaged or ignored figure.

Since that day when I received a revelation of the importance of spiritual fatherhood, I have seen myself as a father to those the LORD has placed in my life, raising them as a father would care for his children.

I want to see all my spiritual children grow and become all that God has intended them to be. I am always ready to encourage them, and I am never afraid to correct them with love. I want the best for their lives, as a father wants the best for his children. There is something so precious, so wonderful, so holy about parenthood.

When my father was alive, I admired him, and now it appears easy to honor my spiritual father. He provided me with stability and security. He always seemed to know what to say. We never lacked for anything. His wisdom for us and his compassion for others was a hallmark in his life. He was a man of integrity. Its effect on my life is evident to this day.

Every man is called to be a father! There comes a time in every man's life to "take their place" and fulfill their spiritual father role. The people around us are crying out for it. The spiritual orphans are out there, waiting for a parent like you to guide them. Begin to see yourself as a father to those the LORD puts in your life.

As men continue to seek the Lord, studying His word, let us live holy lives, and be an example, God will enable us to do for others what He does best for us as the loving and caring heavenly Father that He is.

DEDICATION

I would like to devote this book to my savior, Lord Jesus, who has given all of us to model when we honor our heavenly father. To my biological dad, when he was alive, he taught me life lessons. I miss him every day. He is now in heaven.

To Pastor Joseph Loruis Dessources, who inspired me since my childhood, is such a great example of living a life of faith.

This book is dedicated to my talented and lovely mother, without whom I would be nobody. In the absence of my father, she plays the role of father as well.

To my wife Widza, who always reassures and consoles, never laments, or hinders, demands nothing, and endures all.

To all my spiritual children that I am honored to mentor. Thank you for letting me know that you had nothing but great remembrances of me, for being a part of our wonderful ministry, and for showing up loyalty and honesty.

www.ingramcontent.com/pod-product-compliance
Lightning Source LLC
Chambersburg PA
CBHW022109090426
42743CB00008B/771